With a Great Master in India

With a Great Master in India

JULIAN P. JOHNSON, M.A., M.D.

Radha Soami Satsang Beas

Published by:
Jagdish Chander Sethi, Secretary
Radha Soami Satsang Beas
Dera Baba Jaimal Singh
Punjab 143204 India

Tenth edition 2002

09 08 07 06   8 7 6 5 4 3 2

ISBN 81-8256-036-5

Printed in India by: Lakshmi Offset Printers, Delhi-110 092.

MAHARAJ SAWAN SINGH

Contents

Foreword

First and foremost, this book is a personal expression of a man's relationship with his spiritual Master; a book about love, about wonder, about worship and surrender, a book about the path to God. It speaks of the absolute importance of the Master, the gracious Master who is the soul and very center of all worthwhile spiritual endeavor, whose supreme quality is manifest love, the same quality which is the essence of his teachings. It conveys the living Master as the ideal, the highest and best in actual life, because he himself has actualized in his own person the highest ideals of all religions. The book bears witness to the fact that by emulating such an ideal, the disciple is given a practical path to follow, whereby he too may achieve the same results.

Apart from a brief description of the inner spiritual path, and a gist of the teachings which shaped so gloriously the last ten years of the author's life, the book consists of letters written by Dr. Johnson to his fellow disciples and seekers in America. Julian Johnson was the first man from a Western background to travel to India (which in those days seemed so remote and alien) in order to meet and live with a Master of the Beas line of perfect Masters. In his own words, this book "is a personal testimony to all those who may be seeking the light"—a testimony for which his own personal experience provided the base.

Written during the first fourteen months he spent with the Master, living with him in continuous and close personal association, sometimes in Beas and sometimes traveling through northern India, Dr. Johnson's letters are anecdotal and replete with finely observed contextual detail. Now more than sixty years have passed since the letters were written, and the book stands as a historical record of the changes that have taken place since then in international attitudes and in Indian society itself. Most interesting, however, for the disciple or spiritual seeker, is the way in which the book throws light upon the apparent changes in the relationship of Master and disciple within the context of the Beas tradition of the teachings of the saints.

Every age is characterized by its own particular conditions, and saints and Masters adapt their ways to the specific needs of their times. They come to the world to guide us to knowledge of our true self, and they speak in a language which is meaningful to us. Julian Johnson was already in the latter years of his life by the time he traveled to India. Throughout his rich and varied life he had never wavered in his search for truth, his search for a practical path through which he himself could experience and know truth.

As he explains in the Introduction, Dr. Johnson was initially attracted to Sant Mat through a booklet which caught his eye at a friend's house in California. He read the words: *"The supreme being is a boundless ocean of spirit, or love, and the human being is a drop or current of spirit or love from this ocean; and love being the very essence and means of existence of the whole creation, it follows that no effort in any direction, temporal or spiritual, unless actuated by love or affectionate regard, can be crowned with success, and the work or labor rendered easy, sweet and harmonious."* The words were in absolute congruence with an intense personal revelation he had just experienced, and they marked the beginning of a spiritual journey which led to his initiation by the Great Master's representative in America, and his subsequent journey to

India. The book is his attempt to convey something of the extraordinary quality of life he experienced in the company of his Master; it is the expression of his joy at the fulfillment of those first words which had attracted him—an outpouring of a heart full of gratitude, wonder and awe.

Today, perched at the edge of the third millennium, many readers would be wary and skeptical of admitting even the possibility of a relationship existing of such unqualified love and submission. We find ourselves part of a worldwide material culture of scientific skepticism. Having systematically argued away our heroes and our gods, we can find no meaning or purpose in life, and no basis on which to establish a common rule of conduct to ensure even functional harmony with our fellow living beings. We are trained from early childhood in the refinements of intellectual inquiry, and the age of information has exposed the relativity of all knowledge. The technology of communication is ubiquitous, and such factors have combined to create a fertile ground for pseudo-intellectuals to inveigle their ways into the hearts of people desperate for love and security. In recent years so many false gurus have advertised and sold their recipes for happiness and permanent bliss across every continent, satisfying their greed for material and personal power by exploiting mankind's intense hunger for spiritual guidance and nourishment.

When Dr. Johnson went to India he traveled to a people who were mostly untouched by the great wave of technological progress which was about to sweep across the world. The people he encountered in the company of his Master were largely unsophisticated and uncomplicated; whether they were highly educated or illiterate made little difference to their attitude to the Master and to their lives. Once they had heard the teachings, once they had understood and accepted them, they were able to put their faith and trust in the Master with-

out fear or reservation. This attitude is what Jesus was referring to when he said, "Except that you become as little children, you cannot enter the kingdom of heaven."

Today the seeker of spiritual knowledge must be ever vigi-
lant against exploitation by false gurus; and yet if he is to walk
on the path, he is also called upon to trust and love the Master
as a small child loves the parent. It would appear that the
disciple is faced with an irreconcilable dilemma. But the true
Master of these times constantly encourages his disciples to
see beyond appearances, to look even beyond the beautiful
and gracious form of the Master which we perceive as the
reality, but which in truth is itself a reflection of reality. He
reminds us that everything we see is but reflections, reflections like the light which is cast upon a wall from a mirror
which has itself caught the reflection from the source. He urges
his disciples to look beyond all form, and concentrate their
effort and attention on discovering within themselves that one
and only reality which is the source of all, the reason for all,
the being of all, which is the sound current, the Shabd.

It is the Shabd which is the real Master, and when the
disciple is initiated, he is awakened to this force within himself. Just as the Great Master stood before Julian Johnson as a
living example for his time of the path to God, so the Master
today stands witness himself to the only way which is effica-
cious in the present conditions. Through Dr. Johnson's book
we share the sweetness and simplicity of the atmosphere
around the Master of his times, and we are given a glimpse
of the teachings of the saints in which the living Master of
the day alone holds the key to God-realization, for it is he
who resolves all contradictions by standing witness to God's
hidden ways.

Faith Singh

Jaipur, May 17, 1993

Letter from Sardar Bahadur Jagat Singh, B.A., M.Sc.

PROFESSOR OF CHEMISTRY, LYALLPUR AGRICULTURAL COLLEGE

Lyallpur
Punjab, India
December 30, 1933

The fourteen letters contained in this book, and the statements in the last section, are based upon the personal observations and experiences of the author, Dr. Johnson. He has lived in close contact with the beloved Master for over a year and a half and I regard him well qualified to write on this subject. I wish to say that in no instance has he exaggerated the mastership or other qualities of the Master. If anything, he has rather understated them. We who have known the Master intimately for many years fully believe him to be so great that no human language can possibly portray him as he is. We can never say how great he is. We can only bow at his holy feet and worship in silence, joy, and deep gratitude.

For many years I have watched men and women of all classes, from the coolie up to the shrewdest and most cultured intellects, sit humbly at his feet while he so wisely pointed the Way. We sincerely wish this might be the great good fortune of all who read this book.

Earnestly yours,
Jagat Singh

Letter from Judge Sewa Singh, B.A.

SENIOR JUDGE OF THE CIVIL COURTS, DELHI, INDIA

Delhi
January 5, 1934

Dear Doctor Johnson,

I have read your letters which are going to be printed in the form of a book with great delight. It is wonderful that you have comprehended in so short a time the teachings of Sant Mat. As pointed out by you, the first essential for a student of Sant Mat is the selection of the right Master. You are, no doubt, fortunate in selecting the Master about whom you speak so much in your letters. The greatness of a Master can be better experienced than described. In my opinion your description of the Master, if it errs at all, it errs on the side of incompleteness. He is beyond description.

The doctrine, that souls can only work out their salvation if they come into contact with a perfect Master and learn from him the secret of the Word, is not a new thing. Almost all the religious systems are aware of it. In the Bible the Son is the Master; the Holy Ghost, the Word; and the Father, the supreme Lord. The Vedas, Upanishads and other religious books of the Hindus, and the Koran of the Muslims are full of references to Shabd and Masters who could reveal it to individual souls. The doctrine may sound a little new to the Western mind, but I hope this book of yours will be of immense benefit to them.

Yours affectionately,
Sewa Singh

Letter from Jagmohan Lal, M.A.

PROFESSOR OF ENGLISH LITERATURE AND HISTORY
RANDHIR COLLEGE, KAPURTHALA

Kapurthala
Punjab, India
December 31, 1933

On a hot summer day in June 1932, a serene elderly gentle-man, very different from the average European or American tourist, dismounted from a closed car and entered my house in Kapurthala. I had the pleasure of entertaining him for two days. I noticed that the things usually sought and admired by tourists held no interest for him. He was a typical searcher for the higher realities, for truth. There was evident a deep hunger of the soul in this American traveler.

He and I soon came to know each other well, and when he admitted me to his confidences, I discovered a man of re-markable wealth of experience and extensive study. He is an eminent surgeon, and since his coming to India, many have received the benefits of his surgical skill, even though he did not come here to practice his profession. He had left a flour-ishing practice in America and, probably at the psychological moment, came to India in search of light. Of course this could be found only at the feet of the living Master. For over a year and a half Brother Johnson has been engaged in an earnest study of the Master's teachings, and to the Master he has dedi-cated his life. He has given to the Master love and faith, the two things needed if one is to make the inward journey to higher regions.

Dr. Johnson has had the good luck to meet a real Master,

and his keen and trained intellect and broad experience have enabled him to grasp the teachings quite accurately and assimilate them. I know that he has carefully analyzed every phase of this teaching and weighed its every point. He has not accepted it blindly. He has so clearly mastered the teachings that he is now eminently fit to put the very quintessence of Sant Mat before his own people. Much of it is given in this little volume, and every word of this book is true, to my personal knowledge.

May Satguru bless his efforts, and through him all America and the world.

Sincerely yours,
Jagmohan Lal

Introduction

"When the disciple is ready, the Guru appears," is a common saying among occultists, and is often repeated in the literature. For a quarter of a century the writer kept trying to believe this statement; but he often wondered if it was literally true, or was it just an optimistic expression of those few who had succeeded in finding one. For a quarter of a century he had believed in the existence of the Guru, the Master, the genuine mahatma. God knows there was plenty of need for them. If they did not exist, there was in the economy of human life a decided deficiency.

If one accepts the major premise of a supreme and benevolent Creator whose fundamental nature is love, then he can scarcely believe that Creator would leave untold billions of his children to wander around like babes in a wilderness, unguided, unenlightened and unprotected. If he sent us down into this world for some beneficent purpose, then he cannot fail to look after us and to see that his purposes are ultimately conserved. There simply must be Masters. That is our first and root conviction. They are necessary to any rational order in this world. Without them, there is chaos, only blind drifting, and chance. Nothing but hopes and vague uncertainties, groping speculations. Excepting the Masters and their disciples, there is not a man or woman in all the world who has any certain knowledge concerning the most important problems of the soul, or even of the existence of the soul itself. All the rest only believe, imagine, speculate and preach; only the Masters *know*.

Without the revelations of Masters—living Masters, not the story of Masters written in books, the origin of which no man can tell—without the certain knowledge that they possess, the scientific student is almost driven to the conclusion that man is only a physical structure, beginning with the foetus *in utero*, and ending in the dissolution of death. He may conjure up dreams to please his fancy and feed his imagination, but they are hardly worth his time. Without the Masters there is no provision for the soul of man. If the Creator has made no provision to properly instruct and take care of the spirit, then there is no spirit. But happily we are not left in the dark concerning these things. There are men who know.

To say that the people have a book to guide them is futile, when but a small fraction of the human race has ever had access to any one book, and there is no general agreement as to the value of any book as a guide. To say that they have priests and other religious leaders to guide them is likewise futile, even ridiculous, in the light of the well-known fact that those teachers are practically all in the dark themselves, leading worldly lives and driven by the five common passions, just like other men. Besides, they are utterly lacking in any sort of agreement among themselves as to the most fundamental principles or precepts by which they propose to guide their followers. To say that they have a divine spirit to guide them is only a guess, a dogma. If that were the case, then the whole world would truly be guided aright and the results would be uniform and highly salutary. Spiritual enlightenment would be universal.

So it is evident that this old world sadly needs real Masters who alone of all men can speak from positive knowledge. For that is the one supreme mark of distinction between Masters and all other teachers: they know, all others only believe.

Always one Master on earth

And so it stands out as a vital fact, well known to those who have had the experience, that the great supreme Father in his lovingkindness has provided that there shall always be at least one perfect saint or Master on earth in the physical body, ready to guide all who are ready to go with him. And no matter where on earth a soul may be, even to the remotest islands of the sea, and no matter what his handicap or difficulties, if he makes himself ready for the Master by always doing the best he can under the circumstances, the very day and hour he is fit to stand before the Master and is ready to follow him in the right spirit, as certain as the path of a planet in its orbit, just that certainly will the Master appear and take charge of his pupil. No matter how the meeting is to be brought about—that may be left entirely to the Master. His wisdom and power are all-sufficient, for he is the viceroy of the supreme King, appointed to do that specific work among men. The only concern of the student is to make himself ready.

A long and thorny path

But the way to the Master's feet is often a long and thorny path. Many are the weary years when doubts spring up and the heart grows faint, when hope is no more than a flickering candle to guide our sore and aching feet. It often happens that a person struggles on for years amidst his doubts and perplexities, groping blindly, as it seems to him, when at last, just as he passes a turn in the road, suddenly and unexpectedly he stands face to face with realization. Then he is ready to exclaim with Cowper:

> God moves in a mysterious way,
> His wonders to perform.

A sketch of my life

I was brought up in a most orthodox environment. When I was a boy, the sermons in the Baptist church where I attended, fairly smelled of brimstone, and anyone who was not "converted" and baptized by immersion was pretty sure of immersion in that lake that burned with unquenchable fire. But there were many questions I wanted to ask; only those questions were generally settled by the indignant assertion that the old devil was putting doubts into my mind. As a boy I was reading and explaining the Bible to everyone. There was no mystery about it. Only I found out later that some of my explanations were not to be tolerated. These were quite unorthodox, and everything unorthodox was of the devil. The book of Revelation was one of my favorites. I knew all about it, even though many of the world's greatest scholars never claimed so much. However, only a few days ago I picked up the New Testament and read that portion again, to see if my later studies had thrown any light upon it. I found, somewhat to my amazement, that now I had not the slightest idea of its meaning. I wonder if the writer himself had any clear conception of it.

Licensed to preach at seventeen

At the age of seventeen I was licensed to preach and spent the next seventeen years trying to convince the world that the Baptist church was the divinely commissioned organ of the Almighty for the enlightenment and salvation of mankind. At twenty-two I was graduated from college at Bolivar, Missouri, from which school I obtained three degrees, and was then appointed a missionary to India. That ancient land always held a peculiar fascination for me. As a boy, even the map of India held me spellbound. Now I was sorry for India and would go out and set her right in matters of religion. I was not then aware of the fact that the great men of India were adepts in religion and spiritual science ages before my own country was discovered by civilized man, even when my ancestors were pirates along the northern coasts of Europe. But I was young, optimistic and egoistic. Nothing daunted, I set out to convert the world. But after nearly three years in India, I returned to America with my orthodox egotism a bit deflated. I was like an automobile tire with a small puncture, a little flat, but still going. I had met a few men in India— although they were not Masters—who knew so much more about everything than I did that I was mystified, amazed. Amazed not so much at my own ignorance as at their massive learning. I had come to India to convert ignorant heathen; but by the side of some of them I was still in the primer class. I had my three diplomas tucked away in the trunk and I never showed them to anybody after that. I had gone out to convert the heathen and the heathen had set me to thinking, even if they had not converted me.

I was born with an irrepressible desire for knowledge. At least it was very early manifest. My mother used to call me the standing interrogation point. I just must know the ins and outs of things, the whys and the wherefores. I never could accept complacently what was dished out to me and ask no questions. And this trait of character has often got me into trouble. It has always been quite impossible for me to fit myself into a nice little stall some place and eat my hay along with the rest. First I wanted to analyze a sample of the hay; and that a good horse is not supposed to do. I never could take gracefully to the harness while some archbishop sat up in the chariot behind me with his whip in hand.

Five years of intensive search

Determined to get my feet on solid ground, if possible, in

matters of mind and soul, I entered school again, this time in the great University of Chicago. There I spent five years in an intensive search for reality, graduating in two different departments, one of which was theology. But my graduating thesis was a disappointment to my dear orthodox professors. I chose as my theme, "The Fundamental Principle of the Reformation." I took the position that the real source and inspiration of the Renaissance and of the Protestant Reformation in Europe was the great principle of individual liberty, reborn and now asserting itself, in spite of all church dogmas, both Catholic and Protestant. The fact that a few great Protestant leaders, themselves only half-liberated from the tyranny of dogma, took a leading part in the general awakening, by no means obliged us to ascribe to their teachings the real source of the Renaissance. They themselves were the unconscious agents of a greater and deeper principle, of a far more gigantic force, which was now moving all Europe and the world.

But my beloved professors were deeply grieved that I did not attribute the great awakening to the dogmas of the Baptist church. Their labor of love had been wasted upon me. I was hopelessly led astray by German rationalism. Much was the pity. But as for myself, I was in a worse predicament than a man on the highway with a flat tire. I did not even have a highway. I was utterly in the woods. I had a roll of diplomas, but they were of no use to me. They meant nothing, except one thing—and that is after all a thing of supreme value— they represented a real mental awakening. If a man once awakens from his age-long stupor and learns to think—actually begins to think independently—he has accomplished much. Until that time arrives, it can never be said of him that he is an educated man, no matter how many diplomas he may have won or how loudly the world may acclaim his learning.

I begin the study of medicine

Being now without a profession that I could sincerely follow, I turned to the study of medicine. That at least was something definite with which I could occupy hands and brain. I won my medical degree from the State University of Iowa and settled on the Pacific coast to practice. But in all the years that followed, my interest in spiritual things never slackened. It rather grew more intense. I must have been born under that star. I sought eternally for the real, for the true. But now I no longer sought for it in organized religion. I no longer expected to find it in the great schools of learning. So I became interested in New Thought, in Christian Science, in Spiritualism. But none of these seemed to get at the root of the matter. I found in Theosophy a greater appeal than in any of the rest. It held a keen interest. It surely had glimmerings of the light. But much of it seemed so far away and intangible. Its great teachers wrote learnedly and pointed to masters far away in the depths of the Himalayas, where the Great White Brotherhood controlled the destinies of men. But when I tried to get in touch with some of these great ones, the path of approach always vanished. I took up the study of Rosicrucianism. That also was good. It seemed to point in the right direction. It was deeply fascinating. But in it I could never find the way to the feet of any man who could speak with authority on any of the deeper problems. If they had masters, they were to me quite inaccessible, and I was put off with many vague promises. I continued to flounder about in deep waters. I never seemed quite able to get my feet on a firm foundation.

Finally, during a long course of reading, and especially during the study of oriental philosophy, of the Vedas, the Bhagavad Gita, the Upanishads, etc., the idea of the Master gradually took shape in my consciousness. There was the ideal.

Standing out among all creeds and systems, yet above them all, was the living Master. He represented the highest and the best in actual life. For he had himself actually achieved in his own person the highest ideals of all religions; and, by virtue of that achievement, he and he alone could speak with authority on the subject. And the most appealing thing about the Master was the idea that by following him, any man might achieve the same results and himself become a Master. No one has any monopoly on spiritual attainments. The idea of the Master appealed to both reason and intuition. I was quite sure that if there were no such thing as real Masters, there ought to be. There must be Masters. I became more and more convinced that if I could not find the solution of all my problems in a living Master, then that solution could not be found on earth. Further search would be useless, for I had now explored about everything else that offered any rational promise of light. So I began my search for a Master.

I wrote to everybody in the world that I had any idea had ever seen one. Most of them did not reply, and this list included many Indians who at that time were posing as Masters in America and collecting ready cash for a prescription purporting to make their students into Masters, for so much per head. Those who did reply generally put me off with some vague and indefinite statement. One man who claimed to have spent years with Masters in India replied: "When you become master of yourself, you are in the presence of the Masters." But to one crying in the wilderness, there is not much comfort in that. Once or twice I thought I had found a Master; but on closer scrutiny and more critical study, I had to give up and begin my search all over again. But each time I renewed the search with more zeal than ever. In spite of many counterfeits, the real Master must be found somewhere. Every good thing in the world is imitated and capitalized on by designing men, and the better a thing is the more cleverly it is counterfeited.

I was now convinced beyond a question that real Masters did exist somewhere on earth. Knowing that India has been the reputed home of the Masters for ages, I would have set out for India at once; but after arrival in India, I would have had no way of locating the Master. I had heard of different men who had gone to India in search of a Master and returned disappointed. I believed then, and have since found out for a certainty, that there are millions of people in India who have no knowledge of a real Master, perhaps many who have never heard of one. And I now know of scores of people who live less than three miles from the greatest Master in India, and yet they have not the least idea of a Master. They have seen him pass through their villages time and again. They have heard him spoken of as a "holy man." And yet they have no idea of his mastership. They pass him by as just one more of the thousands of *"sadhus,"* who are more or less revered as men who possess certain unusual knowledge and powers, but most of whom are little more than dirty beggars, going about collecting an easy living. The people have been so imposed upon that most of them pay but slight attention when a real Master does appear. But my search was a long-distance one and I just had to go on waiting and searching for a clue.

A medical officer in the U.S. Navy

In the meantime I had spent nearly three years as assistant surgeon in the United States Navy, during and after the Great War. Later, I settled in California and resumed private practice. I built a hospital of my own and developed a considerable surgical practice. Years passed and a heavy practice wore on me to some extent. But my interest in the eternal quest never abated. I became entangled in world affairs; I made much money, invested it and lost it. Complications, involving business and domestic difficulties, wove about me an intolerable situation. All the while that inner urge for the eternal realities became more and more dominant and insistent. I became more and more disgusted with the world and its false glamours. It seemed to me that the whole world was rushing on, madly indulging itself, and then when it got the belly ache, it came to me for a pill or an operation. I was sick of it all. So one day I rented out my hospital, filled up my gas tank and, all alone, I headed for the south on a vacation. I didn't even tell my most intimate friends where I was going. In fact, I didn't know myself. But I knew I had to have a change and a rest. And a few days later I drove into a grove of eucalyptus trees in Brawley, the Imperial Valley.

The darkest hour of my life

It was then, during the winter of 1928-29, while visiting in the Imperial Valley, California, that the darkest hour of my life came upon me. It seemed as if I had come to the end of all roads, the end of the trail. Ahead there was nothing but the desert, the darkness and the end. Nothing but blank darkness. Bitterness of soul and despair settled upon me. I was ready to hate the whole world for leading me on in a series of constant disappointments. But finally, realizing that would only make bad matters worse, I at last resorted to humble prayer to that supreme Father in whom I had always believed, but who, it seemed to me, had sadly neglected one of his boys. Self-pity and blaming others is such an easy way of sliding out of one's own shortcomings.

An ocean of love

Whether my prayers were heard and answered by some gracious divine agency, or whether my attitude of prayer simply

brought me into harmony with the divine law, does not matter. The end results are the same. I awoke one morning with a
keen realization of having been literally floating in an ocean
of love. It seemed to me an actual experience, floating in an
ocean of love. I could think of nothing else all day that day.
The aspect of the whole world had changed overnight. And
the following morning I had the same delightful sensation. It
was evident that some vital and transforming change had
taken place in me. I looked upon the world with new eyes. I
loved everything that lived; and most gratefully I bowed my
soul before the supreme Father.

The long search rewarded

A few days later the impression came to me like the strokes of
a hammer upon my brain that I must go north. So, without
further hesitation, I just put a notice on my door—"Too hot;
gone north." In fact, the weather was getting pretty warm by
that time. I drove over to Pasadena and Los Angeles, and then
up the scenic coast route. Returning by the inland Pacific
Highway, I stopped in Ashland, Oregon, to visit an old lady,
Julia R. McQuilkin, whom I had known and loved for twenty-
five years. She was then nearing her eightieth milestone in
life's journey. But her brain was active and her soul radiant.
She had lived a long life of useful deeds. Almost the first thing
I noticed on entering her sitting room, lying there on her
library table, was a copy of *Radha Soami Mat Prakash*. It
struck me peculiarly. I began to read, and one of the first para-
graphs my eyes fell upon read:

> The supreme being is a boundless ocean of spirit,
> or love, and the human being a drop or current of
> spirit or love from this ocean; and love being the
> very essence and means of existence of the whole

creation, it follows that no effort in any direction, temporal or spiritual, unless actuated by love or affectionate regard, can be crowned with success, and the work or labor rendered easy, sweet and harmonious.

Strangely enough, here was my ocean of love in which I had been baptized; and in the very same paragraph a complete and perfect explanation as to why I had failed in so many of my undertakings. It came with the force of a personal message from the skies. I continued to read. When lunch was ready, I fed myself with one hand while I held on to the book with the other. I asked questions. Finally when the little volume had been read through the second time, I asked my friend where she had obtained it. In all philosophical and occult literature there was nothing like it. It carried a different message. My beloved hostess smiled and said that it was an exposition of the teachings of a Master in India. I eagerly enquired, which Master? She then told me that for seven years she had been an initiate of this Master and if I wished she would give me directions as to how I might get in touch with him myself. "If I wished." Would I wish to drink water, if I was dying of thirst? At last I was to find a Master. I asked her why she had not told me of her Master before, when she knew well that I had long been in search of one. She smiled again and said: "You were not ready before." Ah, that was it. I was not ready. Even though I had longed to see the Master, I was not yet ready to stand in his holy presence. That was why my Guru had not appeared. We are so prone to think of everything else except our own unworthiness. But at last, thanks to that ocean of love and my good friend, I was to find a Master. About eight months from that date I received instructions from the

Master himself to proceed to Port Angeles, Washington, for my initiation. I could never convey to another person any adequate idea of the deep gratitude which I felt when this message came.

A little over a year from the date of my initiation, one fine day I laid down my surgical instruments, locked the doors of my hospital, and slept soundly that night. The next morning I drove down to San Francisco to take a steamer for India. On the twenty-fourth day of March 1932, I sailed out through the Golden Gate, headed for Honolulu and the Far East.

Studying Buddhism in Honolulu

I stopped over in the Hawaiian Islands for two weeks; but instead of much sightseeing, I put in most of the time studying with a very cultured gentleman by the name of E. H. Hunt, who is an accredited *bhikshu* or priest of the Buddhist faith, in charge of the beautiful Hongwanji Temple. This faith is well known in the Islands, mainly because of the large number of Japanese adherents. But the impression of this writer is that Buddhism, like Christianity, has seen its best days. It has served its purpose in the divine plan, has drifted into formalism, and will eventually disappear, as a more vital faith comes to take its place.

The journey westward

On the fifteenth of April, we weighed anchor and slowly moved out of Pearl Harbor, while the band played the beloved "Aloha." As we sailed away into the setting sun, a gorgeous rainbow formed a perfect arch over the entire city of Honolulu. We accepted that as a hopeful sign, a promise, that our quest would not be in vain, and that we should return to American soil with the fruits of success. Under the tricolors of Mikado, our ship set its steady course westward, while we looked fondly upon the last receding speck of land over which floats the American flag.

Our outbound party

There were in our party sailing from Honolulu five Americans, outbound on four different missions quite as opposite to each other as the four points of the compass. One was a young man, ex-soldier, a lovable, jolly fellow, going to Singapore, or the Philippines, or wherever the ship wished to carry him. His object was to spend time, his youth and money. It mattered not at all if fate brought fortune, romance or war. He would play his guitar under the southern moon and forget that the world had its problems. He couldn't be bothered.

There was another young man of about thirty years of age, educated, affable, and a bit serious. For he had read Kant, Schopenhauer, Herbert Spencer and, of course, Nietzsche and Ibsen. But in Tokyo he easily found the pretty Japanese girls more interesting than the *Critique of Pure Reason*. He was willing to agree with Keiserling that the Japanese had reduced lovemaking to a fine art, and he had always been interested in the best examples of real art. He was going out to Shanghai to build for himself fame and fortune in the newspaper business. As a journalist and writer of philosophical story, he expected to succeed H. G. Wells; perhaps, even blazing the trail into worlds of high thought that Wells had never dreamed of. Such is the boundless optimism and egotism of youth.

There was then a middle-aged couple, husband and wife, bound for Tibet as missionaries. They had been called, so they said, to carry the gospel into that almost inaccessible region which was now the very last outpost of the known world where it had not been preached. This was necessary, they explained, so that in the end those heathen might be properly damned, without excuse for their obstinacy, when the Lord Jesus should come in all of his glory to judge the world. The Lord was at that moment, they believed, somewhere in the highest heavens, all ready with his shining host, restraining his impatient angels, just waiting for the day and hour when he and his wife had crossed to the western border of Tibet, preaching as they went. Of course, they did not know a word of the language which they were to use in preaching. But that did not matter. Then suddenly the end of the world would come—the terrible judgment, the wholesale destruction of the wicked, and the gathering up of the elect. That select and somewhat exclusive company would consist of only a hundred and forty-four thousand, out of the total population of the earth. Of course, they had already received their tickets as members of the select party. All the rest of mankind, since the beginning of the human race on earth, were to be cast into hell fire, with the devil and his angels. Such was the cheerful outlook of our missionaries.

Lastly there was an elderly man, possessing the intelligence and scientific training of the average American surgeon, a contemplative mood, a philosophical bent of mind and somewhat of a dreamer, now going out to India in search of a mahatma—not Mahatma Gandhi.

It is astonishing how our friends suddenly become interested in our welfare the moment we start out to do something which they think we should not do. There are always plenty of people standing ready to whip us back into line with the old order; but seldom is anyone willing to help push us out in search of the new. While my friends in America were getting anxious about me, I was becoming quite solicitous about my missionary friends. They were evidently moving straight toward deliberate suicide, fired with a fanatical zeal worthy of any crusader. They had only money enough to take them to Yunan, and their entire equipment consisted of a few clothes, a roll of blankets, two Bibles, and a guitar which they could not play. They had no organization supporting them, and no sort of preparation for the rigors of the cold mountain regions ahead of them. They expected Jesus to miraculously enable them to speak the language and play the guitar, to feed and clothe them, and to provide means of travel. They were further handicapped by having with them their little boy only five years of age. I wished to save them, if possible, from a fatal error. So, on separating from them at Hong Kong, after trying persuasion in vain, I handed them a letter to be read at their leisure, urging them to reconsider.

While my missionary friends were reading the above-mentioned letter, I was reading many anxious messages from America. The following letter will do for a sample.

Oakland, California
March 26, 1932

Dr. Julian P. Johnson
Care of the American Consul
Hong Kong

Dear Julian: Just received your note, too late to meet you. I was out of town for a couple of days. I was much surprised and shocked when I read it. I cannot feature you doing such a thing and I hasten now to send this letter out, hoping that when it reaches you in Hong Kong, you will have reconsidered the matter and may turn around and come back home. You, an educated man, a skilled surgeon, with many years of experience, a hospital of your own and a good practice—just to drop it all and start out on a wild goose chase? If it were summer time, I would say the heat had affected your head. Mahatmas, Masters? Who ever saw one alive? Those birds exist only in the warped imaginations of dreamers. If there were such men in India, certainly such eminent scholars as Swami Vivekananda and Tagore would know about them. Anyway the Christian faith of your mother, and in which you used to be a minister, should be good enough for you. Why leave the good old U.S.A. in search of a chimera among heathen people, in a strange land and among a million strange gods? It is unthinkable. Come back home and forget it, and settle down and enjoy life, while you may. You have many years of usefulness ahead of you yet.

Earnestly and affectionately yours,
N. W. D.

Affectionate warnings unheeded

I fear much that in both cases the benevolent interference was in vain. Only another instance of love's labor lost. We are all such obstinate creatures. We all left Hong Kong, bent upon our several errands, and nothing but personal experience will ever convince us that we are in the wrong. My missionary friends will probably leave their bones beneath the drifting snows somewhere in the mountain vastnesses of Tibet, unless indeed a miracle should intervene.

And the one in search of a mahatma sails on serenely over the southern seas, bound for India and whatever discovery there awaits him. In the meantime, totally unmindful of either missionaries or mahatmas, the beautiful moon climbs the eastern sky, soft breezes blow from the islands of the south, and the Southern Cross beckons us on to Singapore.

Tonight we stand on the deck of the steamer and watch the restless waves keep time to the silent march of the stars, just as they have done for a million years and more.

The arrival in India

It is no part of the plan of this little volume to describe in detail the long journey to India. The space must be reserved for more important matters. The reader may imagine with what emotions the writer beheld at last the outlines of India. Dear old India. Much-loved and much-misunderstood India. We enter the muddy waters of the Ganges. Calcutta lies on the distant horizon. Our journey nears its end. Slowly we come to anchor at last, and the American traveler sets foot upon the land which holds so much of either success or disappointment for him. The land of Prince Gautama Buddha, the land of the Vedas, believed by many to be the oldest teaching ever recorded by man, but which are quite modern compared with one other; the land of renunciation and ascetic extremes; the land of Ram Chandra and Sita; the land of Kabir and Nanak; the land whence so many world religions have emanated. For even Jesus received his inspiration here. The land of wretched poverty and of immense wealth; the land of pitiful ignorance, and also of the keenest brains, the broadest culture and the deepest wisdom to be found anywhere on earth. The land of a million gods, and also the land where wise men teach earnest students to become gods. Such is India, the mother-land of the world.

The story of him who came to India in search of a Master will now be continued in the form of a series of letters written to his friends and fellow students in America, giving in some detail his actual personal experiences with the Master. The facts set forth in these letters are duly attested by a group of men who occupy the highest positions in the social order.

The reader is at liberty to write to any of them for confirmation of any part of this story.

The last section of this book will consist of a much-condensed statement of the Master's teachings, commonly called Sant Mat, or the teachings of the saints. It is also called the path of the saints, or the spiritual science of the saints, Radha Soami teachings, the yoga of the saints, and many other names. But they all refer to that system which has been taught and practiced by all saints of all ages and countries for countless years. It may be explained that the term *saint* (Sanskrit, *sant)* as used here has no reference to canonical saints, like those of the church. It refers to a great soul who has learned to live a perfect life among his fellow men, who has mastered himself and made himself free from all limitations on the soul, developed his latent powers, risen to the highest pinnacle of achievement in the spiritual realms, and is now able to conduct his disciples to the same sublime achievement. Such is the real saint, or the perfect Master; and such is the great Master portrayed in the following pages.

The Masters adopt modern methods

If it happens to occur to the readers of this little volume that this public statement is not in line with the time-honored method of the Masters, let it be noted here and now that the modern saints have abandoned the old rigid rule of secrecy and exclusiveness. The reasons that made it necessary in past ages no longer exist. The saints now make public appeal to modern intelligence, using modern methods. They freely give out their message through books and public discourses. The only secrets now withheld from the public are certain instructions given to disciples at the time of initiation and during their further progress on the Path; also the individual personal experiences of the disciples. Those secrets, while vital to the student, would be of no use to the public. To all disciples the Master's injunction is: "Freely you have received, freely give. Only do not waste your time trying to give to those who are not ready for it. Use common sense and discretion, tempered with love."

It may be well to call attention to one other fact in this connection. Occult students have generally held the idea that the Masters accept disciples only after the most rigid and searching tests; and so generally the disciples of a great Master have been very few in number. But now their methods are different. Great numbers flock to them. Our Master here, for example, has initiated as many as four thousand and nine hundred in one month. The tests are not severe. Almost all true seekers who come to the Master honestly in search of the Way are accepted by him. In reality the Master accepts larger numbers not because he wishes a larger following, but because he wishes to give to a larger number the golden opportunity of spiritual redemption. No matter if many of them follow but indifferently and die at last straying from the Path. If they have been initiated, the seed has been sown, and in the next life they will be more spiritually minded and make better progress. In the following life they will do much better, and not later than the fourth life following initiation they will, every one, come to the full light.

The full story cannot be told
Having now had the inestimable privilege of living for over sixteen months in close association with one of the greatest of these saints, the writer is most happy to offer this personal testimony to all who may be seeking the light. The major part, and the most vital, of all his experiences with the Master must remain untold. They belong in that category of individual experiences which can never be told to another, and if it could

be told would serve no useful purpose. Only the most superficial, the least convincing, of all his experiences the occult student may put into writing. Each student in search of the larger reality must travel the Path for himself. The most that even the Master himself can do at first is to point the way. If the soul of the reader is ready for the light, he will not fail to see the guideposts directing him on the way; nor will he ever again pause until he rests at the Master's holy feet. But if he is not ready, he must pass again under the Wheel and wait for future ages to bring him to higher levels of consciousness.

The Letters

A series of letters written to friends and
fellow students in America during the
first fourteen months of his sojourn with
the Master.

One

Dera Baba Jaimal Singh
Punjab, India
June 3, 1932

Dr. and Mrs. H. M. Brock
Port Angeles, Washington, U.S.A.

My dear Friends: I am going to write to you the very first letter after my arrival here and the meeting with the Master. All of this experience has made me feel more than ever my indebtedness to you as the Master's representatives in America.

When I arrived in Calcutta, I found four letters from the Master awaiting me, giving me assurances of his welcome to India, and also giving me directions as to my procedure on arrival. He desired me to come directly to him, rather than stopping over to see other places just now. He said he was going to Karachi shortly and invited me to accompany him. Of course, I followed his instructions and, accordingly, sent him a telegram that I was taking the first train out of Calcutta for Jullundur City and Beas. I had only about six hours in Calcutta, and saw but little of that great city. However, that did not matter. I was looking forward to something much better than seeing cities.

It took me two nights and one day, by fast mail train; and so, about six o'clock Thursday morning, June 2, I arrived in Jullundur City, a nice little city about twenty-seven miles from Beas. Two of the Master's most intimate helpers met me at

25

the train. One was his private secretary, Rai Sahib, and the other was Sardar Bhagat Singh, an attorney or advocate in Jullundur City. These men extended to me such a cordial welcome that I soon felt quite at home. The Master's secretary is all kindness and goodness, and the attorney just radiates true nobility and spirituality.

But the greatest of all surprises awaited me as I entered the home of the attorney and stood face to face with the Master himself. They had not informed me that he was there. I expected to have to go on to the retreat at Beas to meet him. But he was so kind as to come on to Jullundur City even the night before, so as to be there to meet me and extend his gracious welcome. The attorney introduced me by saying: "And here is the beloved Master you have come so far to see." But I would have known he was the Master, if no word had been spoken. There is no one like him. I was simply unable to speak, scarcely able to think. I just grasped his hand and stood there. After a while, I was able to tell him that I was most happy to have this privilege of meeting him. I do not know just what he said, but it was something about me being most welcome. It seemed that I stood there in a sort of daze, but quite happy. A sense of great peace had come into my soul. One of the signs of true greatness is that they do not awe you with their greatness, towering above you; but they inspire in you a subtle peace of mind and soul and make you glad.

All about the Master were grouped a number of men and women, some sitting on the rugs, and others actually kneeling in an attitude of worship. Later when I had a chance to notice them, I could see that their faces were literally shining with love and happiness. The Master sat down, after shaking hands with me, and I was given a chair close by him, while all the rest sat on the floor so as to be lower than he was. This was to show their respect for his exalted character.

At length I was able to find speech and told the Master that I was so taken by surprise at meeting him thus unexpectedly, that I was quite unable to express my deep appreciation at having this wonderful privilege of meeting and talking with him. He expressed delight that I had been able to complete my long journey and assured me that he would do all he could to make my sojourn in India as comfortable as possible; but he expressed some concern lest the food and such accommodations as they could provide might not be what I was accustomed to and so might prove a hardship to me. I assured him that material food and physical comforts were of very little importance to me now. I had come to India for that spiritual food which was of much more vital concern. His smile was most gracious and he assured me that he would do his best to give me even that spiritual food as I had need.

First impression of the Master

And now I wish I could really describe him to you or tell you of my impressions. But did you ever try to describe a beautiful sunset? I was expecting to see an unusual man. I knew he had a long white beard. I knew he was an elderly man and an East Indian. The color of his skin is about that of the average American with a good coat of suntan. He is five feet nine inches tall and weighs 128 pounds. He wears a tall white turban and his general bearing is that of natural born nobility. No king could be more graceful and dignified, and yet that dignity is so tempered with sweet humility that one is drawn to him. His voice is low and clear as silver bells. His smile is extremely gracious and one can see that his heart holds loving-kindness for all.

After an hour with him, about all I could do was to just sit and think of his face. I could think of nothing else. I could still feel the vibrating music of his voice. I could fancy the whole environment was permeated by a peculiar light. Or was that a fancy? His followers here do not think that is a fancy. To them he is verily "the light of the world." And that is no exaggeration or hyperbole. Truly, as his secretary wrote several years ago, he is to be seen and not described. Since seeing him I can think of nothing else. His image lingers before me all the while. I have never seen such a face before, nor imagined there was one like it among the sons of men. If ever there was a face combining old age (he is now seventy-four years of age) with beauty, majesty and calm power, it is his. But beyond all of that there is a sort of spiritual radiance which no words can describe, but which gives one a feeling of deep peace, as if the discords of earth were no longer possible in his presence.

As you look into his face you lose all desire to talk, even ask questions. You simply absorb the light. His voice is vibrant with love and his smile seems as if it lights up the room. He is as simple in manner as a little child, with no sort of pose or air about him. He always appears as if he regretted being the center of an adoring crowd. His spirit of good fellowship is enchanting. You soon feel at home with him and not only that, but you come to feel that there is no real home except in his presence. Thus he makes you a part of his own family at once. His manner toward all of us is like that of a mother comforting her tired children and soothing them to rest. His manifest love is his supreme quality, as it appears to me, and that is also the very essence of his gospel.

The spirit of true brotherhood
I had come from the very opposite side of this globe to see

the Master, and now the one hour and a half I have spent with him is more than abundant reward for my long journey. He and the entire group of disciples have given me such a sincere welcome that I cannot find words to express my gratitude. Their love appears to know no bounds. They treat me as if I were truly their own brother returning from abroad. In it all there is no formality of any sort. It is real brotherhood. It is a deep mystery how this has come about. I must have time to think. At present I am conscious only of a deep peace and of infinite gratitude that the supreme Father has directed my wandering feet to stand at last in the presence of a living Master.

At four in the afternoon I bade adieu to our worthy friend the lawyer, and the Master, and left with the Master's secretary for the retreat at Beas. *Dera* really means "tent." It was originally the hermitage of Baba Jaimal Singh, who was Guru to our Master. Now the place is called Dera Baba Jaimal Singh in honor of him. When I left the Master in Jullundur City he was ready to start on a trip across country to visit his sons and other relatives at Sirsa, about 150 miles from here. At the end of the week he will return here and we will start for Karachi, as the weather is now getting quite warm in this section. We came to the Dera in a beautiful Dodge sedan belonging to our Master. I was made welcome by all of the good people of the Dera and was soon comfortably quartered in the guest house. Every attention was given to my comfort. They are all so kind to me, and I simply cannot give them money, not even the barber. They will not have it. They say it is their privilege to serve me as their brother and guest. I wonder if there is another such group of people on earth? I doubt it, even as I doubt if there is another such sublime faith known to man. Here they live their religion. It is their daily bread, their life, from the Master down to the poorest laborer.

A great monthly satsang

Last Sunday was the time of the regular monthly gathering, and over 8,000 people were here, they say. There were 2,000 people applying for initiation, and of that number the Master accepted and initiated 740 souls. And of the total number initiated, two—and they were both women—were able to see inner light during the devotional period which followed the initiation.

Meditation at 3:00 a.m.

You will no doubt be interested and perhaps amused when I tell you that promptly at three o'clock this morning, at the ringing of a bell or gong, I got up and sat for devotion for a period of three hours. It was never so very easy for me to get up early in the morning, unless it was to go to the surgery for an emergency operation. I was always ready for that at any hour of the day or night. But here at the Dera the Master always rises at three o'clock in the morning for his devotions, and he generally sits until six in the summer time, and until eight in the winter. Most of the others do not sit so long. This is not compulsory on anyone; but all do it out of their love for the Master, because they know it is his wish. The Master regards the sitting as the most important of all our activities. After a delightful period spent in meditation, I went to sleep for a while only to be awakened by a bunch of boys who wanted me to go for a walk with them. Among them was a grandson of the Master and a great-grandson, the latter a beautiful boy of about six years. So we went for a delightful walk up the Beas River, just as the sun was coming up over the valley beyond. The river here is perhaps a quarter of a mile wide and it presents a weird and enchanting scene peculiar to this country.

The time passes, and as this letter is already long enough,

I must bring it to a close. I will no doubt have more to write later that will be of interest to all of you. I hope I may thus be of some real service to the American students who may not have this privilege which I am enjoying.

With Radha Soami greetings and fraternal love to each one, I am very happy to be your grateful fellow student,

Julian P. Johnson

Two

Dear American Fellow Students:

In my last letter I gave you an account of my first meeting with the Master. Believing that a further account may be of interest to you, I am going to give you in some detail the story of the last month with the Master. It must be understood in the beginning that I acknowledge my utter inability to do justice to the subject. But I will do the best I can. And I hope in the future to be able to eliminate myself from these accounts; but just now I regret that I am unable to do that because of the fact that I am writing about my own experiences and impressions. These letters are therefore somewhat in the nature of a personal testimony, of which personal experience must form the basis.

The man who brought the message to America

It is the custom of the Master to give daily discourses on some phase of his teaching in public meetings which are called *satsang*. These satsang gatherings are largely attended every day, and at the end of the month many thousands attend. It is then a sort of "camp meeting." There has been manifest the deepest interest and most absorbed attention in all of these meetings which this American has attended. But the weather was getting very hot, some days up to 120°F; and the Master,

with a few others, was getting ready to leave for the coast.
One hot evening we sat on the roof terrace of a building and
conversed for two hours with Kehar Singh Sasmus, the man
who brought the Sant Mat message to America and gave the
instructions to Dr. and Mrs. Brock more than twenty years
ago. He is now gray, with a long beard and a patriarchal appearance, but very active; and his face is full of light and love.
He is so utterly unassuming, humble and kindly that it is a
real benediction to meet him. I said to him, "And so you are
the one who brought this great truth to America and initiated Dr. Brock." Quickly he replied, "No, I did not initiate Dr.
Brock; I only served as the beloved Master's helper. We can
do nothing of ourselves. It is the Master alone who initiates
all souls. He alone connects them with the sound current."

A journey into higher regions

I shall never forget another evening which I spent on the roof
with a small bunch of the Master's most beloved disciples,
and we listened to a lady give a detailed account of her spiritual experiences, what she saw and heard during her journey
through the first, second and third regions, and up to where
she entered the region just beyond Daswan Dwar. The only
trouble with the account was that the interpreters became so
absorbed in the story themselves that they almost forgot to
tell it to me. This was a rare privilege, as disciples are generally forbidden to relate their inner experiences to others. But
on this occasion we had special permission from the Master.
And this is only one instance of how kind and gracious he is
to everyone. It will be impossible for me now to give you even
a resumé of this story. Perhaps some time I may do so. But
it made the journey ahead of us all a more vital and fascinating undertaking, thrilling to the last word. One could see the
light of truth and joy shining in her face as she told in simple

language of the marvels she had seen. But she paused to say that there were no words in earth language to describe many of the things to be met with there. They were utterly unlike anything familiar to earth travelers. But she told her amazing story with such unhesitating assurance of reality that it carried conviction. I believe she has been about fifteen years on the Path and is much loved by all who know her. She appears to be about forty-five years of age. Her name is Bibi Rakhi.

On another occasion a group of disciples sat on the roof and we listened to stories of many kind deeds of the Master in helping students. It may be known to all of you that as a rule the Master does not use his extraordinary powers to perform miracles. But they say that on special occasions, when the disciple's spiritual welfare can be promoted by such means, the Master does extend his grace. It must be well understood that this faith is not built upon miracles, nor is any student to look for them in his own experience. If they come, it is simply his good fortune and the boundless grace of the Master.

Visit to the kingdom of Kapurthala

I would like to give you an account of my visit to the native kingdom of Kapurthala, only a couple of hours drive from Beas, and of the drive through the grounds and visit to the palace—a veritable museum of ancient and modern implements of war, many other historic relics, and the beautiful art exhibits. The *raja* is a lover of art, and some rare specimens adorn his palace walls. But these things can be told by travelers who have nothing more important to write about. I must hasten on with my story of the Master and his work. I may just mention in passing that I was a guest in the home of a college professor by the name of Jagmohan Lal who teaches in an excellent school of higher learning in the capital city of this little kingdom. For two days the most cordial brotherly love and kindness was extended to me in the home of this good man who is a devoted follower of our Master. It was through his kindness that the writer was admitted to the royal palace and grounds.

The Master is thinking of America

One day the Master and a number of the leading disciples were sitting in my room conversing, while I was showing them my diplomas. When I showed the Master my diploma in theology, one of the men remarked that it was my certificate to be a padre. The Master smiled and said, "Now you will soon be a real padre." And when one of the men urged the Master to go to America, this writer said, "Yes, it would be a great day for America, if you would consent to go there and take them the truth." The Master replied, "The work that I would do in America you shall do for me, and that is why you have been brought here to prepare for it."

Love, the supreme law

On the morning of the twentieth I met the Master at the bedside of a sick man. After a few minutes' conversation with the sick man, the Master turned to me and said in English, "Where there is love there is no law." I said, "Yes, because love is the supreme law." And the Master said, "Yes, that is true."

Hard to remain here in the body

One day the Master seemed a bit sad and I asked him if he did not feel well. He said, yes, he felt all right. And then he went on talking about the higher regions, how the soul so much disliked to come back down here and put on dirty rags, when it was used to wearing the finest robes in the palaces of the Father's kingdom. He said, "It is hard to remain here in the body." On another occasion the Master remarked that if one looks down upon this world from the higher regions, it all resembles a bunch of garbage cans and outhouses, in comparison. The very atmosphere seems poisoned and so dark in comparison with the fair lands above. So it is difficult even for the unselfish Master to remain away from home and live in this low land of shadow and uncleanness. Only his great love for human souls who so much need his help detains him here. But there is one great compensation which he has even now. He may daily visit his splendid mansions above and converse with the glorified inhabitants of that region. The joy of that then sustains him through all of his arduous labor here. He knows it is only a matter of time until his work will be finished here and he will take up his permanent residence there.

The Master's eldest son

I must tell you of the visit of the Master's eldest son. He recently came to visit his father at the Dera. He is a fine-looking, large man, now with hair and beard gray, looking to be about fifty years of age. When I was introduced to him, I made the remark that I would rather be the son of such a father as his than to be the Prince of Wales. He replied that he too was very proud of his father, and he added, "He is as God to me." I understand that this eldest son was initiated by the Guru of our Master. The Master's family are all initiates, I am told. On another day when we all met with the Master for satsang in Lahore on our way to Karachi, this same son came to greet his father, and it was an inspiring sight to witness the devotion he manifested. There stood the Master with dignity tempered by a beautiful humility, and a tall, stately old man, with long gray beard, the Master's son, prostrated himself on his knees touching his forehead to his father's feet. I fancied such a sight was rare on this planet.

Ninety-one years a satsangi

I must mention an old satsangi who is a faithful attendant at all of the meetings. He is 109 years of age and was initiated by Soami Ji himself, the founder of this science, some 90 years ago. He is a bit stooped and feeble now, but is able to attend all of the meetings. He walks to them all and sits as close to the Master as he can get. One day I asked him if he was happy and he said, "Oh yes, of course." Day after day he sits, the joy-bells ringing through his soul, waiting patiently for his release. He is very thin. Evidently not much of his time does he put in consciously down here, when he can withdraw from the body and rest in those bright upper regions with which he is already quite familiar.

(It may be added here that he passed to his home above only a few weeks after this letter was first written, and his poor old thin body was reduced to ashes out on the banks of the Beas River.)

The journey to Karachi

At 4:00 a.m., June 23, we left Beas for Lahore, the capital city of Punjab, on our way to the sea coast. This part of the trip was made by motorcar. We stopped over a few minutes in Amritsar where, in the dawning daylight, several hundreds awaited the Master at the new hall. A wealthy man by the name of Shiv Shankar is building a magnificent new hall and quarters for the Master to hold satsang in Amritsar. The Master inspected the work on the new structure and we then drove on, arriving in Lahore at seven o'clock. We found a crowd of about five thousand people awaiting the Master and he gave an hour's talk. After a brief rest and breakfast, the Master went on to a distant village where about four thousand people were gathered to greet him, while the rest of us remained in Lahore.

At nine o'clock the next morning the Master met us at the
train en route for the coast and we went on together.

At about eleven o'clock that morning our train pulled into
a station amidst a great throng of people, many thousands.
They had heard that the Master was to be on that train. He
went out to meet them. They had erected a little platform
and spread rugs for him. The Master never stands up and
lectures to the people, American fashion. He always sits on
the floor or on a little raised platform and, with legs crossed,
talks to them in a conversational manner. His voice is full of
melody and it carries well to a large audience. At this particular station the train was actually held up for about half an
hour by the crowd, while they clamored for the Master's
darshan—that is, just to see him and give him their Radha
Soami and get his greetings. Can you imagine a fast mail train
in America being detained by a mob of five thousand people
pressing to get a glimpse of a minister or priest of some
church?

Again it must have been about ten o'clock that night when
the train stopped and a great crowd came sweeping in from
the platform, almost pulling the Master out of his bed; men
and women all in one grand rush to get near him. They
crowded into the compartment and then the Master went out
onto the platform and talked to them for a few minutes. This
was the last demonstration on the way to Karachi, which we
reached on the morning of the twenty-fifth.

Karachi by the sea
Karachi is a beautiful little city lying along the borders of the
Arabian Sea, about fifty miles north of the mouth of the Indus
River. As we came near the city a strange sight greeted us. An
airport lay out to our left with two modern planes standing
there, one of them with the motor going just ready to take

off. Over to our right was the highway, and on it mingled modern motorbuses, oxcarts, and a long string of camels forming a caravan, such as might have been seen on these shores long before the days of Alexander the Great, or even before the days of Abraham, or the Babylonian empire—ages of history meeting at a single point.

Arriving in the city we were met by friends, and the ever-present motorcar always waiting for the Master wherever he may go. This time it was a Buick and belonged to Devan Sahib, a government railway official who is a disciple of the Master. We drove a few miles through the city and then out into the suburbs to an elevated region by the sea, where we found two bungalows all ready for us. Many friends who had preceded us were waiting to welcome the Master. Here soft breezes blow in from the sea practically all of the time, day and night. Like some places on the coast of California, this little city is rapidly building up as a summer resort. Many magnificent palaces are already built here and others are under construction. The change is most welcome after the heat of the Punjab plains and the dust of the long journey. A bath and breakfast and once more the world seems a fair place to live in.

The Master sits by the sea

And now what shall I say? Am I still on earth, or am I in some weird borderland? And how shall I estimate the values or describe the situation? It is all so strange, so unlike anything in the homeland. It is beyond words. Here we sit by the ever-surging waters of the Arabian Sea calmly watching its whitecaps break upon shores hoary with age and rich in history. We think of ancient religious teachers who have visited this land and probably stood upon this very spot, including Krishna and Buddha and even Jesus himself. For it is known that he visited here. We try to recall some of the doctrines of the ancient sages, prophets and mahatmas; and all the while we are conscious of the fact that the greatest of them all sits on a bench here by us at this moment, calmly reading a book.

We have so often wished that we could have known some of those great souls who were the lightbearers of the human race; and yet right here by our side sits one whose radiance is not dimmed by comparison with any of them. For he has penetrated all the deep mysteries of life and of death and he has conquered the last obstacle between man and the supreme heights. Here by us quietly rests one whose powers, I believe, far transcend those of the greatest prophets of old. And I sit here by the waters of the ancient sea, trying vainly to comprehend the situation.

As I sat there at his feet studying the situation, he looked up from his book and glanced across at the restless waves. Some children played near him and a smile lighted his face as he watched them.

This writer then asked the Master the following question: "When you know so much more than all the books in the world, why do you read them?" He smiled and said, "I wish to familiarize the mind with the writings of the different saints so as to use them in my discourses to support the teachings of Sant Mat. There are many people who look to some old authority which they have learned to revere. We can often take advantage of that to convince them of an important truth."

It is difficult now to fit myself into the picture here. I am an American trained to different ideas—trained in the materialistic West, that West which believes itself to lead the world in all modern achievements. As a product of that West, I sit here at the feet of the greatest of modern sages whose wisdom embraces and transcends all ages and lands. I sit at the feet of one whose powers are not limited by time or space, whose word or will could transform a kingdom or a world, whose very glance has in it the power of death or of eternal life; aye, whose commands even the waves of this ancient sea must obey, if he chose to command them.

And yet he is in outer appearance only a gentle old man, with a long white beard and a kindly smile for the children who play at his feet. The multitudes pass by him, some haughty and vain, not even noticing him, bent on errands of pleasure, pomp and ceremony. But occasionally comes a group of satsangis who bow adoringly at his feet. I listen as he greets them with that sweetest of all pronouncements—"Radha Soami." And so the day passes. All the while I keep thinking, what a pity that the world does not know him. The crowds pass him by as if they were utterly blind, and so they lose the golden opportunity which might have meant so much to them, if only their eyes had been opened.

Glimpses of a marvelous truth

How I wish I could do justice to the subject, but I am as yet only a little child on this holy path. Day by day I am trying to grasp the deeper meaning of this sublime truth, but much of it still eludes me. It is much like an experience I had at Crater Lake, the first time I ever saw it. I went up and sat down at the rim, and for four hours I sat there trying to let my soul grow big enough to appreciate the majesty and sublimity of it all. So I sit today at the feet of the Master, trying to penetrate the deep mystery, trying to open my consciousness to an adequate appreciation of its sublime depths.

Aside from the Master himself, I try again and again to compare this system of truth with other teachings, and daily I am more and more amazed at its solemn grandeur. It is like the peaks of the Himalayas, only a few hundred miles north of us. It is monumental, gigantic, overwhelming. But no man can absorb it all at once. At first there will be doubts and many things will astonish the student. Later he will come to wonder why all the world has not seen its truth and hastened to make it their own. It is so obviously true. After floundering about in a vortex of religious and philosophical speculation for a half-century, I am prepared to welcome this teaching with more than ordinary gladness. When one gets even a feeble grasp of its fundamentals he simply knows it is true. It is so clearly rational and it meets all demands of both reason and intuition. It is a scientific fact and it solves all of the problems of life, here and hereafter; and they are solved in such a beautiful and simple manner that one instinctively knows he has reached the final solution.

And the center and soul of it all is the gracious Master himself, now living among us. He goes on loving and teaching and helping us, leading us up over all the difficult places, up and up, until the last supreme height is reached and we merge our souls into the stream that gave us being, bathed in infinite light.

There is much more one could write, but not now. This letter is already too long. I will close it with a prayer which I believe you will all like. It was written by our first Master, Soami Ji, and was translated into beautiful English by Pingle Rung Rao of Hyderabad, Deccan:

O august Radha Soami,
Thou living Self and loving Master,
Beneficent Father and Mother of all,
Be merciful, make us thine own,
And save us from the snares of time.
Passed I through Sat Yuga, Treta and Dwapar,
Unknowing of the heavenly melody proper;
Now art thou merciful in this Kal Yuga hard,

To chant in loud and lucid strains the Word,
O Soami, descending into this plane below.

Helpest thou the living entities
To span the worldly ocean across;
To cast the trinity off and reach the Fourth Abode
Whence the living Name unfolds,
And the living mastership
Bathed in glory and effulgent light;
Thy servant tenders this solemn petition:
Grant us even the regionless region,
The chief abode, the sphere of bliss,
The refuge at thy feet, my Lord.

                    With greetings of fraternal love, I am
                        Your fellow student at his feet,

                                    Julian P. Johnson

Three

Dear American Children of the Light,

The time has arrived for this disciple to make a further report to you concerning his experiences in India. On the second day of this month, just two months from the day he first met the Master, he made the following entry in his diary:

"For twenty-five years I prayed and longed for the day when I might stand before a living Master. Now, thank heaven, I sit at his holy feet, look into his eyes, listen to his inspiring voice as he expounds to his disciples and others the sublime precepts of his message. I wonder how it has come about and yet it is a living reality. Daily my consciousness becomes more absorbed in this glorious truth, daily more enraptured in the sacred presence of my Lord."

The above entry gives some clue as to my present attitude of mind after two months with the greatest of all teachers. But the Master daily grows upon one's consciousness. No beginner can fathom his depths all at once. Often after years of constant association, the disciple fails to appreciate fully what the Master is. The mind is so stupid, and it has wandered in the darkness so long.

Morning dawn by the Arabian Sea
It is now four o'clock in the morning, on the shores of the

44

Arabian Sea, where this disciple stands. The hush preceding
the dawn is only accentuated by the roar of the waves breaking upon the sands. On the east coast of India the red streaks
of dawn are just beginning to be reflected in the sacred waters of the Ganges. Early pilgrims are gathering for their morning bath. Three hundred and fifty million people are at this
moment just beginning to stir with the activities of a new
day. But the light of this dawning day is material, and it brings
no relief from the wheel of birth and death. The light of the
spirit is not yet shining in the souls of all of these millions.
There the darkness of the ages still broods, and each soul keeps
its silent vigil in the prisonhouse of *maya.** Age after age,
through ten thousand times ten thousand lives, these poor
souls have struggled up through the slime and ooze of earth—
up and up, slowly emerging into the light. And this disciple,
listening here to the ancient song of the sea, while the first
streaks of dawn light up the east, prays for the dawn in his
own soul. In the dim early light he can see the vague outlines
of a bungalow, standing on the crest of a hill; and in that
bungalow at this moment quietly sits the Master in holy meditation. In that the disciple can see the hope of India and of
the world. For the hope of the world, the light of the world, is
the living Master.

The Master always busy
Since the last letter this disciple has lived, apparently, many
years of ordinary life; so much of thought and experience has
been crowded into one short month. Indeed, after wasting
millions of years, it is highly expedient that we should concentrate much activity into what time is left. The dear Master

---

**Maya:* the illusory quality of the phenomenal universe wherein everything is
subject to change and destruction. This is the great illusion which obstructs
man's vision of God, the real, the eternal.

gives satsang twice a day to all disciples and enquirers besides many private audiences. We all try to spend as much time with him as possible, and his patience is never exhausted, listening to questions, some of which must appear trivial and silly to him. Yet he always has a kindly answer for every one. He prescribes spiritual remedies for all our spiritual ills. He is the "great physician." People continue to come from all directions to see him. He came here for rest, but they will not let him rest. The little informal talks in the sitting room have grown into gatherings of two to three hundred. Many of all classes and creeds come to see and hear the "holy man." Some out of curiosity, some to argue, and some to seek the truth.

Only two weeks ago an overenthusiastic leader of the Sikh religion came and tried to involve the Master in arguments. Later his fanatical followers started opposition meetings nearby and some of them came and tried to create disturbances in our meetings. The police had to be called once to dispel the mob and restore order. Every inch of ground is bitterly contested. The science of Sant Mat is much opposed all over India, wherever it is preached, because it destroys the old superstitions and interferes with the livelihood of the priests. It is particularly opposed by the Sikhs whose fundamental faith is practically the same as this, but they have given up the idea of a living Master and have bound themselves to the sacred writings alone. This fatal mistake of theirs no doubt came about through a misunderstanding of some remark made by their last Guru just before his death. Anyway, they now denounce all living Masters although their sacred scriptures teach the vital importance of a living Guru. This is a very peculiar phenomenon in the history of world religions.

But in spite of all opposition, Sant Mat is rapidly spreading. Having started publicly in 1861, it now numbers something like a quarter of a million adherents. It may be said with truth that this is not really a religion in the historical sense of that term. It has no creed, no priests, no ceremony and no outward show of any sort. There is only the Master and his disciples. That is all. The system itself may be called "the science of connecting the soul with its Creator." That is the Master's own definition. It is the practice of the sound current, through a scientific system of concentration and meditation. It is not concerned with any external forms. It establishes no external authority. The individual simply follows the Master, as the student of chemistry would follow his instructor in the laboratory. It is a universal science and is worldwide in its application to human needs. It is suited to all nations and peoples. It is the only religious or spiritual system ever inaugurated in history that is absolutely universal in its application to the religious needs of mankind. And while it is not actually a religion in the historical sense of the term, yet it amply satisfies the deepest religious needs of the soul; and in uniting the soul with its Creator it accomplishes the *summum bonum* of all religions. It answers to the noblest aspirations of the finest spirits among men.

All classes wait upon the Master

It is quite interesting to note the personnel of the Master's disciples. Just yesterday, out of a gathering of about three hundred, we noted sitting meekly at the Master's feet, listening to him with rapt attention, four doctors, six college professors, five lawyers and judges, including one supreme court judge, and a considerable number of others, probably eight or ten, who have degrees of master of arts, doctor of science, bachelor of arts, etc. It must be a marvelous message indeed that can appeal to such men so strongly and at the same time appeal with equal force to the lowly and the ignorant. While they cannot follow the scientific aspects of the system, they absorb the spirit of it in their souls and so reach the goal at the same time as the learned and the great. It is a blessed thing that the ignorant can love as well as the learned, and it is love that takes the soul up.

Wherever the Master goes, he is loved and honored alike by all. At his holy feet all meet on a common level, and all worldly distinctions are forgotten. Even rajas have bowed before him and sought to make gifts to him. But the Master accepts no favors from anyone, high or low. He remains always the giver himself, never the receiver. He insists that his mission in this world is to give and not to receive. In that respect, as in all others, he is our great exemplar. A few days ago this disciple attended a rich lady in sickness at her home. The husband gave him twenty-five rupees for the charity fund, as reward for his medical services. But the Master ordered the money returned, with the message that we want only the love and goodwill of the people and not their worldly goods. Where on earth is there an equal to this?

Two important things learned
If you ask this disciple what is the most important thing he has learned during these two months spent with the Master, the answer must be that two things have taken prominent positions in his consciousness.

The first one is *the supreme importance of the Master.* This great truth grows upon one as he advances in the study. He finds more and more that the Master is the very center and soul and substance of the system. Without him there is nothing. And this means that he must be a living Master—not one of past ages. It is in this respect that all of the prevailing world religions have made their fatal blunder. It is the reason why they have become devitalized, a dead formality, a lifeless shell. No soul can ever be saved from the clutches of maya and the wheel of birth and death without the aid of a living Master. There is no other way and there never has been any other way for a single soul to escape. Without the personal intervention and help of a living Master, no one now or in any past age has ever been able to shake off the bonds of mind and matter and rise to higher regions. We are all utterly dependent upon his grace for our liberation. Without him each soul is as dependent and helpless as a newborn infant. Left to itself, it would surely perish.

The Master illustrates the situation by comparing us all to people in frail little boats out on an angry sea, each by himself struggling on against inevitable death in the storm-lashed waters. There is no possible escape. But in the midst of the struggle, a great ship hoves in sight and the captain calls aloud to all in the angry waters below that they may come aboard the ship and he will take them safely to port. The captain is the Master and the ship of salvation is *Nam*, the sound current. But in spite of the fact that death is certain if they remain where they are, yet very few accept the gracious invitation of the captain. This is because they are laboring under the deceptive delirium of the physical senses, deceived by the god of this world. The conclusion of the whole matter is that all systems of religion or philosophy which do not make the Master the keystone of their structure must be discarded and the living Master must be sought, as the very first and most vital concern of the individual.

What is a real Master

In spite of the fact that he had believed in the existence of real Masters for a quarter of a century, this disciple did not have a very clear and definite idea of what a Master is until he had contacted one. It is believed that occult students generally do not have a very clear conception of the Master. Of course, the whole world is more or less familiar with the general idea of a mahatma, rishi, Guru, or Master. They are generally thought of as great men who have "attained," who have realized "superconsciousness," who have miraculous powers. Men and women talk and write learnedly of mastership. The Masters are conceded to be great and unusual men. But when we are told that a true *Satguru* or Master is in fact the Lord Creator himself, now and here, operating in a human body, the student is somewhat startled, to say the least. Many will be ready to throw up their hands in protest. How can it be? And yet if you reflect but a moment, you will see that the Master could be nothing else than just that.

We speak of oneness with the divine. Unless that is a mere rhetorical flourish, it must mean what it says. And actual oneness with the infinite means identical individuality. Hence the Master who has attained that oneness with the infinite Lord is now identical with the Lord. He is the Lord. We speak of a spirit of oneness among groups of individuals; but that involves no organic oneness. It is a mere figure of speech. But the case is quite different where individual men attain oneness with the supreme being. In that case they actually blend their very beings with the Supreme. They thus partake fully of all of his attributes. So the lesser becomes identical with the greater, one and the same being. That is the goal of all development. It is beyond the highest heaven of poetic fancy or of prophetic vision. And that is exactly what the Master has attained. That is exactly what has made him a Master. The exercise of his divine prerogatives is limited only by the human body in which he resides, and the laws governing the life of that body.

If one objects that this exalts the individual man too highly, it may be replied that it exalts the whole human race along with the Master. If he be a god, then all men are potential gods. They are in fact gods already of a lesser degree. If the Master is the supreme Creator operating in the human body, then all men are sparks of that same central fire. An illustration may help us to grasp the idea. The concept of oneness is fundamental to the occult student for he must lose himself and not only come "in tune with the infinite" but must become one with the infinite. If we take a common electric bulb of fifty-watt power and let it stand for the average man, then we may compare the Master to one of fifty-thousand-watt power—although, of course, the proportion is not correct. But the light in both is due to the same electric current that comes from the same central dynamo. Manifestly the only difference between the two lights lies in the amount of concentrated energy and power and the intensity of radiation. In both cases latent universal energy has become dynamic. Each one is a part and parcel of the same universal essence, but it is not all of that essence.

So, the Master is the Lord himself, but he is not all of the Lord. For the infinite Creator is universal spirit. He becomes dynamic in individuals, and thus sheds his holy radiance among men. The Master manifests the Lord, but he does not manifest all of the Lord in this one human body. Likewise the ordinary man is a spark of the divine essence, but he has not yet developed into that glowing, radiating light that the Master has become. But the disciple looks confidently forward to the time when he also shall become a Master, when his light shall shine equally with that of other Masters. And that is the glorious outlook of all students on this path. All about us here at the Dera are men and women who are well along on the Way, and the joy of attainment even now illumines their faces. To lead the disciple to the goal of mastership is the work of the Master, and without the Master, no one can ever attain mastership. It is utterly impossible. Hence the vital importance of the Master in the Sant Mat system.

Egotism our worst enemy

The second great truth so strongly emphasized here during the last two months of intensive study is the fact that *egotism is our worst enemy*. It is the most stubborn and difficult force to be overcome before we can make progress on the inward path. And it is also the last one to die when the disciple has fought his final battle and stands on the very threshold of perfect realization. This is one of the five deadly foes that seek always to enchain us to the Wheel. It can be overcome only by the gracious help of the Satguru. Here again his vital importance to the student is manifest. Without him we struggle in vain against these five deadly enemies of the soul. They are the chief agents of the negative power, under the direction of the mind, to keep us bound to earth.

We leave Karachi tomorrow on the return journey by way of Agra. We should have some very interesting things to report in our next letter.

With fraternal love and best wishes
From your brother at his holy feet,

Julian P. Johnson

Four

Beloved Children of the Dawn,

Greetings from the beloved Master and from all satsangis in
India. How we wish you could have been with us during the
past six weeks. Many and varied have been the experiences.
The delightful breezes of the Arabian Sea were a blessing to
soul and body. But the time came to leave the coast. It appears that while time is no item in the successive ages of the
soul, yet to this short-lived body time seems always to be
crowding us. The Master and party left the coast for
Hyderabad on the tenth of August, this disciple remaining
behind to look after a sick member of our party. He then
rejoined the Master two days later in Hyderabad where we
were all entertained in the elegant home of Devan Sahib, an
executive officer in the North Western Railway. He is of course
a disciple of the Master. This is Hyderabad, Sind, to distin-
guish it from Hyderabad, Deccan. It is a beautiful little city
lying along the banks of the Indus River. Here the Master as
usual held satsang, attended by enthusiastic crowds.

Satsang in Hyderabad, Sind
At the first evening satsang held here an old man insisted on
arguing with the Master, although he had been an initiate for
over thirty years. This is something that is almost incompre-

53

hensible. How many human beings who have accepted the Master as a Master can then sit down and argue with him is one of the deep mysteries to this student. Later this man came to ask advice of the Master, claiming that he had never been able to go inside, or to get any satisfactory results from his meditations. Of course not. How could he expect results? He was manifestly suffering from one form of that deadly malady—egotism. It is a disease that manifests itself in more forms than neurasthenia. Anyone who can bring himself to contradict and argue with a Master surely has that disease in a malignant form. How could he expect to go inside? He may never hope for spiritual success so long as he has it. Happily this sort of thing is very rare among satsangis in this country. A beautiful humility is the rule, so far as this disciple can see.

Along the banks of the Indus
August 13, we accompanied the Master for a ride over the city and out to a park on the banks of the Indus River. The river is now quite swollen from rains and from melted snows high up in the Himalayas. This river is probably two thousand miles long and at this point is about three-quarters of a mile wide, although in the deep mountain gorges it narrows down to sixty feet or less. We walked down the riverbank for a short way, close by its turbulent waters, and this disciple wondered how many mahatmas had left their sacred footprints along its shores during the slow-moving centuries. Like the Ganges and the Jamuna, the Indus has long been considered a sacred river by some of the native people.

The old city of Jaipur
August 16, we went on to Jaipur, a native kingdom, where members of the party were entertained in a lovely home of an old satsangi. When we went to leave this place after two

days' delightful visit and rest, this disciple offered his thanks to the host for his kindness. But he replied, "I am not the host. That is the Master; he gives everything." And that well illustrates the attitude of the average satsangi. They regard the Master as the giver of all good.

Light shines in the darkness

One afternoon we visited the old and long-abandoned palace of this kingdom. It was built some five hundred years ago and is now only a magnificent pile of ruins in weatherworn marble.

In the midst is a temple to the goddess Shakti, to whom formerly even humans were often sacrificed, but now she gets only animals on certain festivals. As our Master stood before this ancient temple of idolatry—he, the very acme of modern intelligence and spiritual illumination—this disciple recalled the biblical reference to Jesus: "The light shineth in darkness; and the darkness comprehended it not." That was equally true at the moment where we stood. As we were about to leave these splendid ruins, a huge monument of vanished empire and faded glory, we paused and looked back for a moment. The old palace is on a mountain top, and in the days of its glory was quite a fortress. Across the valley, the green and purple of hills and sky mingled with the red and gold of a beautiful sunset. The Master turned and said to the young doctor who was acting as our guide and escort, "One who goes inside will see many palaces, rare and beautiful buildings, landscapes, gardens and all sorts of scenes vastly more beautiful than any that an earthly raja ever built, or that man ever saw on this plane." As he spoke his voice was tender as that of a father and in his eyes was light not of this world.

The birthplace of Krishna

Late in the evening we took a train for our next stop at

Mathura, the birthplace of Krishna. To all orthodox Hindus, this town is as sacred as Bethlehem is to the Christian. Our party took a third-class compartment, the Master refusing to leave his disciples for greater personal comforts. He never thinks of himself and is quite indifferent to physical hardships. So the dear Father had his bedding unrolled and lay on a hard bench, this disciple having the good fortune to be placed on the bench alongside of the Master, only a board between us.

As the disciple lay there during the long hours of the night, he found but little inclination to sleep. He was trying in his inmost being to realize the situation in its right proportions. By his side lay the human form of the Lord of vast regions of light. He lay there so quietly, so utterly unpretentious, so humble; and yet in those bright upper regions so familiar to him, and through which he travels in the utmost splendor, his very garments are more gorgeous than any royal purple, and wherever he goes untold thousands bow down to him as their lord and king. Notwithstanding all of that, here tonight he humbly rests on a hard wooden bench in a third-class railway car, while it rumbles along through the darkness and the dust. It is almost too much for human thought. But we know it is a literal fact.

The Master's keen sense of humor

The next day as we rode along in the jostling old car, the Master told a story of some foolish weavers who had a rickety, noisy old cart. One day when it ceased to make as much noise as usual, they concluded that it must be dead. So they stopped by the roadside and actually cremated the old cart, throwing the iron parts, as bones, into the river. The Master laughed so heartily that it was a joy to us all. In fact he is always jolly and full of fun. He never fails to see the humorous side of things. He and his closest disciples laugh and joke much and there is seldom a dull moment. All are happy and have a good time. There is no long face in the crowd. And why shouldn't they be happy? They have infinite wealth and power. Their lives are no longer limited to this land of shadow and trouble. They can rise at will into regions of unclouded splendor. They are the beloved sons of the great Father and they have only to ask what they will and it is theirs. And the beauty of it is that they know all of this to be true and are now in possession of it. It is not something to be dreamed of as a far-off inheritance. And it is not a matter of faith. They have it now, and they know it. And so they are the happiest people on earth. Their job can never be put into words, and it is quite incomprehensible to the average man of the world.

Sunset on the Jamuna River

We arrived in Mathura on the morning of the twentieth. Here are many interesting places, all sacred to the memory of Krishna. The city is situated along the west bank of the Jamuna. The one thing long to be remembered in connection with our visit to this place was the boat ride across the Jamuna River at sunset. The beloved Master always does things the right way and at the right time. When our party was told to get into a small flat boat, this disciple had no idea of what was coming.

The boat was pulled upstream along the shore for some distance, and then pushed off and allowed to drift across and downstream to the opposite shore. The river here is about a quarter of a mile wide. The scene grew more beautiful every moment. Now we could see the city spread out along the western shore. The sun was nearing the horizon and the most gorgeous colors streaked across the sky. It was one of the most beautiful sunsets ever witnessed. No artist could paint it. Deep

red and gold clothed the low-hanging clouds in glory, changing into purple a little higher up and finally shading off to
pale lavender and light blue, high up in the sky. At last the
sun dropped down below a purple curtain and suddenly
spread out upon the river a great sheet of gold. This disciple
sat at the feet of the Master as he watched the sun go down at
last behind the city. The Master sat quietly talking to a few
enquirers concerning the way to approach the inner worlds.
His face was suffused with a holy light which was more beautiful than that of the golden sunset. Someone remarked to
the Master of the great beauty of the sunset colors. Glancing
towards the west for a moment, he said, "Yes, it is much like
the colors in Trikuti, the second region."

As we drifted across the river toward the city, whose lights
were now beginning to be reflected in the rippling waters of
the river, a disciple remarked to the Master that he wondered
how many real mahatmas had crossed this river since first it
began to flow. He smiled and said, "Many." And some of us
believe that we had the honor and privilege of crossing that
river today in a little flat boat with one of the greatest of all
Masters who have ever crossed the sacred waters of the
Jamuna.

The fire-waving ceremony

As we drifted back across the river toward the city, the gorgeous sun slowly vanishing, the dark mantle of night dropped
over her, and then ten thousand lights seemed to suddenly
pierce the shadows. Our boat was finally drawn up to shore
just beneath an old temple where a fire-waving ceremony was
about to begin. A sort of pyramid-shaped light was formed
consisting of many smaller lights. This was held up by a priest
and waved back and forth. The Master explained that this
was a sort of crude imitation of the light to be seen in

Sahasradal Kanwal, the first station on our inward journey.
But the priests have long ago lost all knowledge of its origin
and inner meaning. The Master said he had brought this disciple here that he might get a look backward into the remote
past of the Hindu religion. Krishna was born here perhaps
five thousand years ago; or it may be ten thousand. The Vedas
had their origins in those times and in them little is said of
the higher regions.

Light again shines in the darkness
Our next visit was to a magnificent temple in the heart of the
city. It has an imposing marble front, floors and columns. It
cost vast sums of money, all contributed by devotees, and is
now a source of a very handsome income to the priests. For
all who enter its sacred walls must pay, and it is constantly
thronged by visitors. But they refused this disciple admittance
although the other members of our party assured the priests
that he was of the same religion as themselves. Evidently the
pigment in his skin was not sufficient. Afterwards the Master
laughed and said next time they would doll me up with some
paint and a turban. This experience only confirms the old
statement that one must be born into the Hindu religion. He
cannot enter it by conversion. By conversation with the priests
at another time, it became evident that they could not give
any reason for this attitude. It was simply the established custom, and that was the end of all argument. To the Hindu,
custom is the one law that cannot be broken.

The others reported that as soon as the Master entered
the temple, word was quickly passed around that a holy man
was present and dozens of the worshippers came and prostrated themselves before him, leaving their idols. Then hundreds more stood in respectful attention while the Master
spoke to them briefly of the way to go inside and see for them-

selves all of the lights and worlds that are there. Even the priests forgot their collection of money from the visitors and stood at attention listening to the Master's words. He told them of the sound current by which alone men might rise to higher regions and gain eternal life and freedom from the wheel of birth and death. It presented a strange spectacle. There stood the real Master in the very center and heart of orthodox Hinduism, expounding his message of light, while both priests and devotees forgot all else as they listened to him. It was another instance of the light shining into the darkness, this time at the most sacred point of ancient Hinduism. Whether any of them comprehended or profited by that light, we could not say. But this we know, the Master never idles away his time, not even in sightseeing. When our party had witnessed this inspiring demonstration, they understood why the Master had visited this old temple of the gods. To him it was not just a sightseeing trip, but was a part of his mission to disseminate the light wherever men walk in darkness.

Master's message to the Brocks

We have not yet reached Agra, the main objective of our trip. Much of interest has already been omitted, and yet this letter has reached its limit. The rest must wait until next time. This letter cannot close, however, until a message from the beloved Master has been recorded. He desired to express his appreciation of the long and faithful service rendered by Doctor and Mrs. Brock of Port Angeles, Washington, on behalf of Sant Mat and the American students. He sends to them particularly his love and blessing. Every disciple now on the Pacific coast, and their fellow student now in India, owes to the Brocks a debt of eternal gratitude. It has been through them that most of the others have received the light since it was first taken to the coast by Kehar Singh Sasmus over twenty years ago. And to this noble soul also we are all greatly indebted.

Sant Mat disciple most fortunate

This disciple wishes profoundly that it could come within the power of human words, either spoken or written, to convey a proper sense or estimate of the wealth we have come upon through initiation into Sant Mat. But the story can never be told. It must be experienced in the innermost depths of the soul. You should permit nothing to ever cause you to deviate from this shining path. Full realization will come in due time, and perhaps sooner than you expect. Suddenly some day the golden glory will dawn upon you and then you will not need to have any man tell you aught of the path. The little spark that now draws you on will have become the infinite light, flooding all your souls with unutterable joy.

Cordially, your brother at his holy feet,

Julian P. Johnson

Five

Beloved Satsangis in America,

We left Mathura by motorbus on August 21 on our way to
Agra. Seven miles from Agra, we paused to see the tomb of
Akbar, the Moghul emperor.

The tomb of Akbar
There it stands in solemn and lonely grandeur within sight of
the ancient Moghul capital. It was built by the emperor's son,
Jahangir. While not to be compared with the Taj, yet this tomb
is a magnificent structure: beautifully inlaid walls in multiple
designs and colors surrounded by tall minarets and, in the
midst, the mortal remains of the greatest of the Moghul rulers. From the top of this monument we had our first glimpse
of the Taj Mahal standing seven miles away on the banks of
the Jamuna River. We are now in a region famed in history.
Here the ambitions of man led him to unparalleled heights
in the achievement of empire, the amassing of treasure, and
the building of splendid monuments. But these monuments,
now weatherworn and faded, their immense treasures scattered and gone, are all that is left of the vast empire and the
glory of Akbar and Shah Jahan. It would seem that here the

genius of man had made his supreme effort to immortalize himself in piles of marble. And here also the vanity of such an effort is most apparent.

Two opposing forces

As this disciple saw the beloved Master standing in the dim light before the black and silent sarcophagus of Akbar, it occurred to him that right there in his presence were two of the most illustrious examples in all history of the two great opposing principles in nature—destruction and construction. The one, representing the principle of destruction, sought to build up himself into empire and glory at the sacrifice of tens of thousands of his fellow beings. At his feet he forced millions to cringe in abject submission and fear. But now all that is left of him and of his vaunted power are a few decaying bones encased in marble.

The other, embodying the principle of construction, is a genuine superman, a real prince among his fellows. Having achieved the greatest conquest possible to human beings, namely, the conquest of self and the emancipation of his own soul, he now seeks in utter forgetfulness of self to rescue others from the downward stream of birth and death and to lead them to the supreme heights of immortal life and happiness. The empire of the one, built upon force and bathed in blood, has vanished from the earth and his bones molder among its ruins. But the empire of the other, built upon love, shall endure when the earth itself is dissolved.

In Radha Soami Bagh

We arrived in Agra at three-thirty and put up in Radha Soami Bagh, in rooms once occupied by Baba Jaimal Singh, our Master's Master. Close by these rooms they are building an extremely beautiful monument in white marble to the memory of the first great Radha Soami Master, Soami Ji. When completed, it will in some respects rival the world-famous Taj Mahal itself, for in simple beauty and elegance of structure it would be difficult to imagine anything superior to it.

We meet a nephew of Soami Ji

Soon after our luggage was unpacked and we had washed off some of the dust of travel, our first visit was to the bedside of Seth Sahib, a nephew of Soami Ji, now seventy-four years of age and in feeble health. This was the real objective of our Master's visit to Agra; for there is a very close bond of love between the two, and it would appear that the end of the earth life of the one is now approaching.

Two real saints meet

The meeting of these two great souls was something beautiful beyond the power of words to describe. It was one of the supreme moments in the life of this disciple. The small group who were fortunate enough to witness this event stood in reverent silence while our Master approached the bedside of the other and with folded hands bowed at his feet. This disciple was quite accustomed to seeing thousands bow at the feet of our Master, but never before had he witnessed the Master himself bowing at the feet of another. By this sign we knew at once that here was no ordinary man, and never did our Master shine more brilliantly, never was his own divinity more apparent, than in that beautiful moment when he bowed at the sacred feet of another saint. This disciple felt that the event he was now witnessing was of even world importance, and he sensed that perhaps in the far off heavens of light that event carried deep significance.

This great soul says he has never taken a morsel of animal food in his life. He was initiated by Soami Ji sixty years

ago, and almost from childhood he has been devoted to Sant
Mat. He says that now Soami Ji himself visits him daily, bringing blessing and good cheer. Meeting with this great soul was
to this disciple a real benediction, and will always be remembered with gratitude.

Model industries in Dayal Bagh

Next day this disciple visited the "Model Industries" in Dayal
Bagh, presided over by Sahab Ji, the leader of the large Agra
satsang. These industries are quite remarkable, actually manufacturing many of the most useful articles of daily life and
putting out a very superior product at a reasonable price. They
incidentally afford employment to a great many satsangis.
They conduct a dairy on modern lines, whose equipment and
management are equal to the best in America. They are making skilled workmen of thousands of men, a thing much
needed in India.

The Agra Radha Soami group

The Agra group of Radha Soami disciples is not connected
with the Radha Soami movement in the Punjab, presided over
by our Master, except by the ties of a common brotherhood
and a similar teaching. There is amity and cordial good fellowship between the two groups and their leaders.

An American satsangi in Agra

At Dayal Bagh, Agra, this disciple had the pleasure of meeting Mrs. Elizabeth Bruce, an American satsangi, who, so far
as he knows, is the only other American in India devoted to
this science. She is a very clever and brilliant woman, making
herself useful in some phases of the industrial work of the
center, while she seeks light on the inner path. This disciple
took lunch with her twice and enjoyed some hours of pleasant

conversation. It requires no little courage for an American woman to leave all of her friends and a successful business in the homeland and come out to India to devote herself to a spiritual science quite strange to all her people. But Mrs. Bruce appears to be very happy in the pursuit of her spiritual ideals in Dayal Bagh, and we wish her all success.

The old Agra Fort, and Shah Jahan

In the afternoon we visited the old Agra fort, now held by the British, of course; and then we visited the old palace of Shah Jahan, the builder of the famous Taj. After a long reign over a vast empire, the building of the Taj Mahal as a monument to his favorite queen, Mumtaz Mahal, and many other noted structures including the Pearl Mosque and the Peacock Throne, Shah Jahan was imprisoned by his own son Aurangzeb, who then usurped the throne. After seven years of imprisonment in a small room adjacent to the Pearl Mosque in this palace, his strength about gone and realizing that his end was near, the old emperor begged that he might be taken to a small porch in the palace from which, looking across a bend in the Jamuna River, he might get one more look at his beloved Taj. His request was granted and he beheld with much emotion that magnificent monument, shining in all of its glory. It is said that on seeing the Taj, the old and heartbroken emperor collapsed and died right there. Thus ended so pathetically, in the year 1666, one of the most picturesque characters in history. He passed from earth as a victim of one of the strangest freaks of fortune ever manifested.

It is told here that once when Shah Jahan was at the height of his world power, he was visited by a spiritual Guru who admonished him about certain things, whereupon the king laughed at the Guru and asked him who could interfere with the emperor. The Guru replied that "the words of the true

Guru are always fulfilled, even though the greatest of emperors has to be made to eat like an ox in the field." And it so happened that during his imprisonment Shah Jahan was taken for a ride one day into the country. Passing a field of gram, he asked his guards to get him some of the grain. The guard refused, saying that he would endanger his own life by doing so, without the emperor's orders. But he offered to lead the camel into the field, make it kneel and himself go away to attend to other matters, leaving him to get the grain himself. But his hands were tied so he could not get the grain, and he had to content himself with kneeling and eating like an ox. When he had done so, he suddenly recalled the words of the Guru, his heart was softened and real faith entered his soul.

The great Taj Mahal

The next day this disciple visited the Taj Mahal. Many books give elaborate descriptions of it. Perhaps the best one will be found in the Stoddard lectures, so no attempt will be made here to describe it. It is sufficient to say that it is, no doubt, the greatest, most beautiful, most artistic and the most expensive structure ever built by human hands within the period of known history. And it is equally certain that no such structure, or anything like it, will ever again be attempted. It is said to have required the labor of twenty thousand men for a period of twenty years to complete it. The whole world was explored for materials. Extensive portions of the Koran are written into the walls, making each letter of black stone and then inlaying them into the white marble. Many beautiful designs and pictures in wonderful colors are made by inlaying precious stones and costly gems into the marble walls. The building is nearly all of white marble, even the floors of the extensive courts and promenades surrounding the Taj itself.

Majestic as it is, after three hundred years, the Taj Mahal

stands today trying pathetically to defy the crumbling hand of time, as only one more memorial of the perishable nature and vanishing glory of all things human. To this truth the Taj will continue to bear testimony until its last marble column has returned to dust.

Crowds continue to greet the Master

August 25, we left on our return trip to Beas and the Dera. Every hour or two all through the night, as the train stopped at the various stations, crowds gathered to see the Master. At the capital city of Delhi a carpet was spread and a chair placed for him. Hundreds gathered around him and listened to a few cheering words, and then he gave them his parting "Radha Soami."

We arrived in the Dera the next morning at nine o'clock, where a crowd of several hundred were waiting to welcome him home, showing the utmost joy and devotion. It is always a great delight to see the beloved Guru again.

Many had already begun to arrive ahead of us for the monthly satsang. So, on Friday the twenty-seventh, probably 3,000 were present at satsang. The next day the number had more than doubled, and on Sunday the Master was greeted by a multitude of 12,000. Loudspeakers were installed so the entire crowd could easily hear the Master's voice.

Many hundreds initiated

Following this meeting the Master initiated 571 souls, after deferring the usual large percentage of applicants. During this gathering this disciple was with the Master in an upper story of the Master's house. The Master stood by the window for some minutes, watching the crowds. Many had grown weary and dropped to sleep on the ground all around the compound.

Hundreds of others stood about in small groups engaged in conversation. The Master turned to this disciple and asked him if he had ever found anything greater than love. He then quoted one of his favorite sayings: "Where there is love there is no law."

The divine mystery of love

And what is the divine mystery of the love of a disciple for his Master? It is one of the most absorbing themes of discipleship. It is something without a parallel in the ordinary walks of life. What is it? How can it be explained? What is the mystery of that holy bond which makes men and women even in the hour of death utterly forget all earthly ties and cling to the Master alone? Fortunately this is one theme upon which this disciple can speak from personal experience, although he is well aware, perhaps because of that experience itself, that he can never give adequate expression to this theme. Since coming to India, this disciple has been blessed with the daily companionship of many disciples whose devotion to the Master has written one of the most beautiful pages in the story of his life. Not only these, but the abiding devotion of the Master himself to his Master adds interest to the theme and crowns the relation itself with undying glory. It is a sacred bond that, once formed, is never broken and its divine fragrance never diminishes through unnumbered years. But like other features of this holy path, the essence of it cannot be written down in words. It cannot be described in human language. To be understood, it must be experienced.

This disciple has seen hundreds of men and women waiting at the Master's door, even at the outer gate, waiting during all the long hours of the day and night, just for one look into his face and to hear his voice in one word of blessing.

Only last night as this disciple came down from the Master's rooms about ten o'clock, he witnessed a sight that would touch the heart of any man. Four flights of stairs leading to the Master's room on the top floor of the hall (in Rawalpindi) were literally lined with men and women, crowded close together and standing, some women holding infants in their arms, all waiting the possible chance that the Master might again come downstairs and they might thus be near enough to have his darshan once more. And this will continue, hour after hour, until at last the word is passed around that the Master has retired for the night. Often the dear Father continues to see and talk to these people until midnight or later, and then he gets only two or three hours sleep; for he rises at three o'clock, or earlier sometimes, to engage in spiritual devotions, or leaves the physical plane for his work in the higher regions. And so he continues until six o'clock in the summer and eight in the winter. It is love on the part of both Master and pupil which the world knows not of, and it is quite beyond their understanding.

The writer has seen men and women of all ages and degrees of culture, sitting in satsang from one to two hours, listening to the Master's discourses, their eyes sparkling with keen delight and frequently tears of joy trickling down their faces. One day he watched an elderly man of sixty years or more as he sat listening to the Master. He scarcely moved his eyes from the Master's form, and for over an hour the tears constantly dropped from his cheeks while his hands remained closed in an attitude of profound adoration. And this was a cultured man, retired from the medical service of the government. Only last night in satsang, a man of thirty-five years, educated, refined, and very wealthy, sat listening to the Master while occasionally the tears dropped freely, apparently unnoticed by himself, so absorbed was he in the light of the Master's presence.

This is a relation almost too sacred to write about; but the following extract, taken from his diary, will be suggestive at least. This writer is deeply conscious of his own unworthiness, yet infinitely grateful to the Master for his lovingkindness.

"October 5, 1932. Now, on the eve of our departure for Rawalpindi, the beloved Father enquired after all plans and arrangements, and ordered a change in the plan regarding my servant, so that he could remain with me tonight and help me in the morning. Bless his holy name. No earthly father was ever more kind and solicitous even of the material comforts of his children. How can I bless him enough! If only I could serve him better. How has he become my very life? It is a deep mystery, but an infinite joy. And how has this heavenly mystery come about in my life? It is so out of the beaten paths of ordinary experience. If the uninitiated were to read this, they would probably assume that the writer was a mooning girl sighing for the lover. To the average Westerner it is quite beyond understanding. But all who have themselves walked this holy path know well that in all the world there is no relation so close and so sacred as that between Master and pupil. There is no other relation so crowned with the frenzy of divine joy. When the disciple feels that every ray of light that radiates from the Master carries with it streams of life itself, he must love him. When he realizes in the depths of his being that the Master is the embodiment of the supreme essence, now engaged in recreating the disciple after the image and likeness of the ineffable Lord, then he knows that life without the Master would be an insufferable calamity. So his thought is always of the Master. In fact, he would say in the words of Bulwer Lytton: 'Not to think of him were the absence of thought itself.'"

With affectionate goodwill, I am
Your brother at his sacred feet,

Julian P. Johnson

Six

The Dera
November 10, 1932

Dear American Fellow Students,

October 6, at 4:00 a.m., we left the Dera again for our trip to Rawalpindi and the mountain stations. The journey was made by motorcar, and was very delightful. Much of the country in the north of the Punjab, and in the foothills of the Himalayas, is similar to that of the California mountain regions. It makes the writer feel quite at home.

Arrival at Rawalpindi

The Master stopped in Lahore for a short satsang at seven o'clock where several thousand people were waiting for him. We then proceeded northward along a very beautiful highway, much of it being shaded with trees on both sides. We stopped at one village for a short talk from the Master to a small bunch of people, and then arrived in Rawalpindi at 2:40. This is a nice little city of about fifty thousand people, lying at the very feet of the great Himalaya range and adjacent to the Northwestern Frontier Province. It is an important trading center. Not far away lies a fertile valley, the seat of an ancient civilization dating back far beyond the beginning of authenticated history. The valley was invaded by Alexander the Great, the Greeks leaving their records, statuary, coins, etc., which have recently been recovered by excavations. This valley was once the bed of a great inland sea, something like the Imperial Valley in California.

The satsang hall in Rawalpindi

On our arrival in Rawalpindi we went directly to the new satsang hall, recently built by Raja Ram, a banker and manufacturing jeweler. Of course, he is a devoted satsangi of our Master's fold. The hall cost about one hundred and fifty thousand rupees. (At the present time [1932] the purchasing power of the rupee in this country is fully equal to one dollar in America, although the rate of exchange is now close to four rupees to the dollar.) This hall is a very beautiful structure; the only drawback to it is the fact that it stands in the midst of the city, surrounded by all sorts of buildings. The furniture is modern and excellent. It has just enough of the oriental in design to add beauty and grace. The Master's rooms are delightfully arranged in two suites, one on the third floor and the other on the fourth floor. The satsang hall, or auditorium, is on the ground floor, but has only limited seating capacity—less than two thousand. At the several meetings held here by our Master this hall was packed, galleries and windows were full, many stood in the streets near the rear entrance, and others filled the main streets in front.

The Master, with his secretary, Rai Sahib, went to his rooms in the satsang hall, while the rest of our party was comfortably quartered in the home of Raja Ram and his wife. They are planning, as soon as the Master gives consent, to turn over all business to his brothers and come to the Dera to live, building for themselves a new house there. They would thus devote the rest of their lives to spiritual things. A great many satsangis look forward to a complete retirement from worldly affairs and coming to the Dera to devote the remainder of their lives to the Master's work. But the Master does not encourage or permit this until they have discharged all their worldly responsibilities.

At the very first satsang a great crowd greeted the Master. This is a privilege they do not have very often. The early morning satsang was also attended by an immense crowd; and then after satsang and all through the day numberless individuals and committees sought interviews with the Master.

The great leper asylum

After the first morning satsang this disciple enjoyed a visit to the great leper asylum in this city, one of the best in India or the world. Here a large number of the victims of this dread malady are cared for. Contrary to popular opinion, the physicians and attendants have no fear of contagion. Here the patients receive the most modern treatment, including chaulmugra oil, which was once thought to be a specific cure, but is now considered to be only a help, many patients making excellent improvement by its use, while others show little improvement. Some are actually cured and discharged, while others remain for life. This is a disease still under scientific investigation and experiment. Many phases of it still elude the investigator. One peculiar feature of leprosy is its very long incubation period, extending from six months to twenty years between the time of exposure and the onset of the disease. No certain and definite cure has been developed thus far. Most cases are self-terminating, and leprosy itself seldom ever kills. There is practically no suffering with it even though fingers and toes may be lost. The patients in this institution seemed quite cheerful, and the management deserves much credit for the kind and efficient service they are giving to many unfortunate men and women afflicted with this disease.

Climbing the mountains

After a few days in Rawalpindi we started for the mountains at 5:00 a.m. on the twelfth. Presently we found ourselves driving along over a good road built by our Master himself over thirty years ago, while he was in government service. That fact, together with the increasing beauty of the scenery, added zest to the trip. Just after dawn, while the Master waited for the second car to overtake us, this disciple decided to walk on alone, as the air was now quite chilly and the exercise would do him good. Anyway, he wanted to walk a little distance over the road his Master had built.

We are now actually in the foothills of the majestic old Himalayas, but their snowy peaks lie yet a hundred miles or more to the north. The air is already lighter and cooler. The traveler begins to feel a sense of exhilaration, also of deep peace, so characteristic of these inspiring old hills. Finally, just as the sun rose over the mountain tops, pouring a flood of gold down the valley, the Master himself came along and picked me up in his car. We began the long climb up the slow grades.

At eight-thirty we stopped at Abbotabad, a small mountain town, and took breakfast. Several scores of devoted disciples of the Master greeted him here, and among them were a goodly number who had worked with him in the old days. Their love for him was quite manifest. The writer was served with a breakfast of rice, warm goat's milk, dates, grapes and pears. The journey was then continued four miles further in the car at which point we mounted horses for the remainder of the trip, the climb of fourteen miles further up to Kalabagh. This was by order of the Master, as he said our party could better enjoy the scenery that way. But some of us suspected that the Master did not deem the motor trip up the steep mountain grades altogether safe. The road is barely wide

enough for the car, and many are the sharp turns, with a yawn-
ing precipice of from one hundred to one thousand feet
straight down below. The grades are very steep, some of them
are apparently twenty to thirty percent. It was not built for
automobiles. All of this road was built by our Master and it is
a masterpiece of construction work. Much of it is cut out of
the solid rock in the mountainside. The ascent was indeed a
pleasure rarely enjoyed. A little over halfway up we paused at
a watering place prepared by our beloved Master, so that all
travelers over this way, whether man or beast, might drink
the purest of cold water.

We are climbing rapidly. The more or less desolate and
barren mountains of the lower altitudes now give place to
pine-covered peaks that tower above deep and colorful gorges.
Rich undergrowth abounds. Ferns and wild roses and dai-
sies, and a few scattering violets, cover the slopes. The air
grows lighter; our ears tell us that we are in higher altitudes
than usual. Three miles below our stopping place, a group of
fifteen men met the Master, a committee who had come on
foot that far to welcome him. This committee grew to a hundred or more by the time we reached the end of our journey.
These mountaineers easily kept pace with our horses up the
steep grades, mile after mile. In fact some of our own party
did the same thing, walking the whole of the fourteen miles.
The Master sat majestically on a spirited young horse, erect
and princely as any raja, the picture of grace and dignity, as
we climbed the steep grades. Many were the times in years
long gone by that he had made this same ascent. He is quite
at home in the mountains, either on foot or on horseback.

Kalabagh, the black forest
We rest in Kalabagh. The name means black park or forest. It
has a small British population connected with the military

establishment. The town lies on the mountain slopes at an altitude of between eight and nine thousand feet above sea level. The scenery is beautiful, some of it really grand. We unpack our luggage at last in one of the most sacred spots in this region or in all of the Himalayas—a little stone house built by our Master and still belonging to him. It has to be approached on foot for some distance. It stands on a point of jutting rocks at the very brink of an almost perpendicular precipice two thousand feet in height. From the edge of the stone-rimmed little yard in front of the house, one can look almost straight down for nearly half a mile, and at the bottom of the gorge runs a little stream of water looking like a silver thread through the purple shadows. Sitting ten feet from the stone wall of the yard it appears as if the yard and house were suspended in midair.

To get a little clearer view of the situation, if one stands on the crest of the mountain above the little town of Kalabagh and looks southward, he will observe a valley many miles long, east and west, something like a mile wide. The walls of this rise to a height of probably three thousand feet above the floor of the valley; and right in the midst of this valley, rising abruptly from its floor, is a ridge about two thousand feet in height. This ridge is connected with the north wall by another ridge, something like the cross bar of the capital letter T. Over this cross ridge we have access to the great central ridge and to the Master's house which stands on the extreme eastern promontory of that ridge.

Looking away across the valley in any direction, one may observe what appear to be stair steps on the mountain slopes. They are little gardens made by digging into the mountainsides, one above the other, and thus leveling little strips of ground upon which these mountaineers raise their vegetables. The houses are made by digging into the mountainsides, extending the roof outward, and then covering it with dirt and gravel. In the winter time these little houses are often covered with ten to eighteen feet of snow. They are frequently abandoned at that time of the year, and the inhabitants go down to lower altitudes until the return of spring weather.

Morning dawn in the Himalayas

October 13. It is now early dawn. We stand upon the rock-rimmed heights overlooking the deep gorge. Two thousand feet below us the lingering shadows hold everything in their dark embrace. But far above us the sun begins to cast a roseate glow over the mountains.

> The highlands catch yon Orient gleam,
> While purpling still the low lands lie:
> And pearly mists, the morning pride,
> Soar incense-like to greet the sky.
> —Burton

At last its dazzling rim looks over the tops of the distant pines, and a new day is born. We could fancy that Shakespeare, escaped from his dull and foggy island, stood on these heights when he exclaimed:

> But look, the morn in russet mantle clad,
> Walks o'er the dew of yon high eastern hill.

The scene is altogether enchanting. No words can describe it, and no mortal artist could paint it. The hush of solemn grandeur adds to the spiritual inspiration of the place and the hour. It is the sacred hour of the mahatma. It is the holy hour of divine worship, and none the less sacred because the call to worship is in a temple not made by hands. Its walls are the mountains and its dome the sky, and the light of the sun points to the worlds of light within. One instinctively thinks of the old yogi morning salutation to the giver of all life:

Hail, hail, to Him alone
Who is the one, the primal,
Pure, eternal, immortal, and
Immutable, in all ages.

For a hundred thousand years and more, these mountain trails and wind-swept pines have frequently heard this salutation. Here men have long sought to unravel the deep mysteries of God and of the soul, and here the disciples of the living Master still seek the calm retreat that enables them the better to meditate upon the holy path. Here many a soul struggling upward, striving to rise above the dark chasms of mind and matter, has found the light eternal. As this American stood upon the jutting rocks close by the side of the dear Master and looked into the dark valley below he instinctively prayed that he might someday be permitted to stand by the side of this same gracious deliverer upon the radiant heights of Sach Khand. He longs with an inexpressible yearning for release from the dense and chilling fogs of the spiritual lowlands. Too long he has groped his uncertain way through the dark and poisoned atmosphere of ignorance and passion. Gracious Master, open to us the gates of light.

Satsang in the mountains

At ten o'clock the disciple sat in the little yard by the Master, enjoying the welcome sunbeams and listening to the great teacher as he talked to a group of old mountaineers—all satsangis now, literally worshipping the Master. Some of them had worked with him in government service thirty or forty years ago. But to them all, now he is the Great Mahatma. They lovingly address him as "Maharaj Ji." This means something like very great and honored sir, though I think there is no exact English equivalent. One old man could scarcely talk from excess of emotion, as he gazed lovingly at the Master and asked many questions. It had been several years since he had seen the Master.

One o'clock, and the Master rests. But the silent worshippers continue to gather in the yard. A group of women sit around the rim of the yard, waiting patiently for the Master to come out. One by one others quietly join them. Old men bent over their canes come one or two at a time, having laboriously climbed the steep trails in order to sit at the Master's feet. Satsang was held at two o'clock on a small level area just above the little stone house. About four hundred had gathered to see and hear their adored Satguru. These mountain folk are a sturdy people. Many of them having descended from tribes who lived by marauding and highway banditry, they now live in an atmosphere of spiritual peace and of steadfast devotion to Maharaj Ji, for whom they would readily lay down their lives.

The Master, a mountain climber

After satsang, just as the sun sets behind the distant purple hills, we all follow the Master for a little walk and climb over the hills westward, along the crest of the ridge. He inspects a proposed site for a new satsang hall which may be built by next year. The ground has been purchased for it. While some of the middle-aged members of our party pause for breath and hesitate as they climb the steep trails, the Master steadily climbs with firm, unfaltering step. And when the summit is reached he shows not the slightest signs of fatigue. Talking and laughing, he is king of mountain and valley alike. He is always Master in every sense of the word. His quick wit, keen intelligence and physical vigor are quite astounding in one of his patriarchal appearance.

Teaching the children.
October 14 at 8:00 a.m. The Master has twenty-three children, sons and daughters of satsangis, seated in a semicircle in the yard, and he is teaching them the position in which to sit and listen to the sound current. They are not given the names. But instructed in this way, they can better join with their parents during the hours of meditation. He says many of them will come to hear the sound current before the time comes for the regular initiation. The Master compares little children to blank paper, clean and white, nothing in the way to obstruct their upward progress; and so they quite easily come in touch with the sound current and the upper worlds. It is only when the minds of the older people are filled with the filth and illusions of the world that it becomes difficult for them to approach the higher regions.

Leaving the mountains
It is a little late in the season for this altitude. The nights are cold. Sudden wind and hail storms sweep over the region almost daily now, and so we must leave before we are overtaken by a snowstorm. On October 18, we descended to Abbotabad, a charming little military station. This is one of the extreme outpost stations of the British military forces in the Northwestern Frontier Province. It is not far from the famous Khyber Pass, the entrance to Afghanistan. Here the Master held satsang for three days, and as usual was greeted by hundreds of enthusiastic satsangis and others. There seems to be no remote corner of jungle or plain, in all of northwestern India, where our Master is not known and loved. Time and

again as we traveled over far stretches of country we were met by groups of men and women waiting for him by the roadside. In many remote villages he paused for a short sat-sang, where scores and hundreds of enthusiastic disciples welcomed him. In one mountain town the Master was greeted by more than a thousand people. Here came also the Sikhs, creating disturbance, advancing their old argument against a living Guru. In this town we visited a place made sacred to our Master and all satsangis by a visit from Baba Jaimal Singh, holding satsang here back in the nineties.

The Taxilla museum and Buddhism

Our next stop was at Taxilla, where is situated a government museum containing many relics of the long ago, recovered from buried cities nearby: pottery, gold and silver ornaments, silver vessels, coins, Greek and Buddhist statues. This disciple, visiting the place as he did in the company of our own adored Master, took particular notice of the large number of statues depicting the Buddha in attitudes of spiritual meditation. The making of statues has always been a favorite method of mani-festing devotion by the Buddhist disciples. Here again we are forcibly brought face to face with another historical phase of old world religions, namely, that of the inevitable tendency to externalize the religion and to forget its spiritual content. We were also reminded of the way men and things grow sacred in the public eye by the lapse of time, while they completely ignore the real gods, the living Masters, who walk in their midst today. One is reminded of the familiar couplet, regard-ing the great Greek poet:

Through which the living Homer begged his bread,
Seven cities claimed great Homer dead.

Here in the museum of ancient relics are scores of statues of the immortal Buddha which, after the lapse of twenty-six centuries, hundreds of millions of men hold sacred; and yet there are, we believe, men who have reached a degree of spiritual enlightenment above and beyond that attained by the Buddha while he was on earth. This we say not to minimize his attainments nor to detract from his sacred character. For in our hearts we bow, and praise him forever. We say this rather to encourage the living disciples. Besides our Great Master, we have a large number in the Dera satsang who already have gone very high in the spiritual regions, for that also is well known here among us, by the grace of our Master. Others are reaching those heights all of the time; and you and I are expected to reach them, not in some future age, or in the next or fourth incarnation, but here and now. If Buddhists were to honor their Lord by taking up the course of development under a living Master, it would not be long until they could meet and talk personally with their beloved prince in his present home.

As this letter has already grown too long, I must bid you good-bye, wishing you all the blessing and love of the Father.

Your brother at his holy feet,

Julian P. Johnson

Seven

Dear Fellow Travelers on the Path,

On our return from the mountains, October 24, we stopped and spread our lunch, camp fashion, by a little stream at the famous Panja Sahib around which an interesting legend has been woven. The stream runs close by a small mountain, on the top of which, the tradition says, used to be a spring of cold water.

By the side of this spring sat a Muslim fakir in meditation. It was in the time of Guru Nanak, in the fifteenth century. It is believed that one day Guru Nanak with one of his disciples came along and the disciple went up to ask water of the fakir, but was refused. Upon hearing this, Guru Nanak thrust a stick into the ground and a stream of cold water burst forth at that point. At the same time the stream on the mountain ceased to flow. Seeing this, the fakir was very angry and rolled a great boulder down the mountainside, with intent to kill Guru Nanak and his disciple. But the Guru simply put forth his hand and stopped the boulder as it came near him. The print of his hand was left in the side of the rock, and those fingerprints are shown to the traveler to this day. The Sikhs have built up around it quite a place of pilgrimage, and are just now laying the foundation for a large *dharamsala,* or *gurdwara.*

From there, we came to Rawalpindi which we reached at three-thirty in the afternoon, and the good Master sought a little rest as he took refuge from the ever-pressing crowds by going to his own suite of rooms in the new satsang hall.

We come now to one of the most peculiar problems in the religious life of India. The Master's return to Rawalpindi was hailed with delight by large numbers. Even a considerable body of the Sikhs who do not follow the orthodox majority welcomed the Master and pledged him their support. But equally demonstrative was the opposition. The orthodox Sikhs did not like the enthusiastic support the Master was receiving everywhere, and so they decided to interfere. They held private meetings and took counsel among themselves as to what could be done, just as the Scribes and Pharisees, leaders of the Jewish orthodox body, did when Jesus became too popular to suit them. They decided to break up the meetings at the hall.

So this evening they came out in force, many of them carrying the customary short sword and some few had long swords. If they had to fight they would be ready. Of course, the Master's disciples were not armed. Two of the visitors sat at the writer's left, and they had long swords which they laid down at the very feet of the Master. Soon after the meeting opened, one loudmouthed gentleman arose in the hall and began to argue and speak ill of the Master. He would not heed kindness or listen to reason. He could not be stopped. So they started to eject him from the hall. This was the cue the others were waiting for. The two at our left took up their swords. Others went to the assistance of the first disturber. For a time the scene grew threatening, but fortunately someone had finally called the police force; and by the time the melée had developed into a mild battle, the police had arrived, and our armed brethren had all suddenly disappeared. They had vanished through the nearest exits as if by magic, and quiet was soon restored.

It is interesting to note that the Master had foreseen this disturbance and had advised the management of the auditorium to have the police on watch. But they had neglected this precaution and, as usual when the Master's advice is not heeded, they came to regret it. In the midst of it all sat the Master, the only calm one in the house. This disciple had taken up a position close by the Master's side, saying to himself that he did so in order to help defend the Master in case of a personal attack. But it may be that subconsciously he felt that near the Master was the safest place for himself. (Since returning to the Dera, the Master has told us that all during the confusion his own Master stood by his side, clothed in light and unlimited power, and that it would have been utterly impossible for anyone to have hurt him.)

After order was restored, the Master quietly announced satsang for seven o'clock the next morning, although he had not so intended before. This was held as announced and all was as quiet as a night on the Potomac, a deep peace pervading the assembly. And so there is the peculiar problem above referred to—that of a section of the orthodox Sikhs and their bitter opposition to Sant Mat. Even the Muslims are much more friendly, many of them seeking initiation of the Master. It may be of interest to note that our Master himself was born a Sikh, and so are a great many of our leading satsangis.

It should be borne in mind that there is nothing in Sant Mat to antagonize any religion, least of all the Sikh religion, the spiritual core of which is practically the same as ours. It has no dogmas to defend. It has no priesthood to be supported. It does not fight any other religion. In fact, it is not a religion in the ordinary meaning of the term. The Master says, "It is the science of connecting the individual soul with its

Creator." It desires to set up no new creed or church and cares
not for the destruction of any old one. With them all it has
nothing to do, any more than a science like astronomy has to
do with a church creed. It teaches the sound current and the
method of yoga which takes the soul inward and upward to
spiritual regions and to ultimate freedom. With this alone it
is concerned. Consequently a devotee of any religion may avail
himself of it without antagonizing his own organization. It is
a private matter and has to do only with internal practice.

Let us briefly sketch the history of Sikhism. That religion
was founded by Guru Nanak in the fifteenth century, and
partly in the sixteenth. Guru Nanak was a real saint, a great
and holy man, who had attained the highest regions. His
teaching, along with that of his contemporary saint, the great
Kabir Sahib, and later Tulsi Sahib also, laid the foundation
for the Radha Soami system of practice. As already stated
above, the basic spiritual core of Sant Mat and the Sikh teachings is practically the same. Soami Ji of Agra only simplified
the earlier teaching and gave it out in clear and lucid terms in
the local language. The yoga or practice of the sound current
is the central theme of them both.

Guru Nanak had nine successors, each in turn carrying
on the great work in the face of much opposition and deadly
persecution. That line of Masters included Angad Dev, Amar
Das, Ram Das, Arjan Dev, Har Gobind, Har Rai, Har Kishan,
Tegh Bahadur, and Gobind Singh, in the order named. Guru
Nanak was born in 1469 and died in 1539, and the last of his
successors died in 1708. The city of Amritsar was founded in
1572 by Guru Ram Das; and in 1588 his successor, Arjan Dev,
completed the famous Golden Temple in Amritsar.

Under the leadership of the tenth Guru, the Sikhs became
a power in the land. They were finally successful in helping
to overthrow the last remnant of Moghul tyranny and to estab-

lish religious liberty under the Khalsa rule of the great Maharaja Ranjeet Singh. As warriors, they came to be known as lions—the word *singh* meaning "lion." They were strong, brave and clean-living men. And today among them are to be found the finest specimens of physical manhood in Punjab or in all India. They offer perhaps the world's finest example of what a noble type of man can be formed by clean living, free from meats, alcohol and tobacco, and inspired by a certain knowledge of the future of the soul in regions of light. Theirs was a noble heritage indeed.

In the course of time, however, the emphasis of the teachings gradually shifted from spiritual practice under the guidance of a living Master to the practice of rituals and external observances. Many devout Sikhs began to confine their religious activities to reading and reciting the holy book, little realizing that it enjoins upon the readers the necessity of internal practice of the sound current to attain ultimate salvation.

October 24, we arrived in Jhelum. This beautiful city lies along the banks of the Jhelum River, one of the five rivers of Punjab. And in this large and fertile area, so well watered, our Master lives. Punjab is doubtless the finest part of India. In Jhelum our Master has about two hundred disciples. As a father looks after all of his children, so our Father tries to visit every section where his spiritual children live. It may take him two or three years to get around to them all, but he neglects none. One thousand people attended satsang this evening. The attention was perfect, as usual. All hung upon the Master's words as if they realized that those words carried the message of eternal life. This disciple, in attending public meetings for sixty years, has never known a speaker who could hold his audiences with such rapt attention and eager interest as our beloved Master can do. And the interest never seems to fail or decrease up to the last moment of the hour and a half or two hours during which he speaks to them in an ordinary conversational manner. Though frequently rising to heights of true eloquence, there is never any attempt at oratory. Everyone feels that his discourses flow from a great heart of love and a brain illuminated by the light of divine wisdom.

We left Jhelum the next morning for Lyallpur, stopping at several places along the way where the Master held short satsangs. Groups of from fifty to several hundreds were waiting for him at many places. Arriving at Lyallpur, there were five or six hundred gathered for satsang. They were nearly all members of the college faculty and their families. Here is one of the greatest agricultural colleges in the world, its experimental farms extending for miles. It is doing much for all India. The beloved Sardar Jagat Singh, who has long been the Master's secretary and writes the American letters, is professor of chemistry in this college. We were entertained in lovely homes and this disciple was served the most delicious fruit salad he had tasted since leaving America.

The next day we came on to Lahore where the Master held satsang at one o'clock, which was attended by more than two thousand people. When we went to leave there, lines of people had formed two blocks long, through which the Master's car made but slow progress. Every man, woman and child was anxious to get one more nearby glimpse of their beloved Satguru. Many had tears in their eyes as they said the last "Radha Soami."

The next stop was in Amritsar, at four o'clock, where a thousand or more devoted disciples awaited their Master. He gave them a brief talk and then, after a short business conference with some judges, lawyers, etc., concerning some public works of interest to the Dera, we started on the last lap of our return journey, arriving at the Dera at about six-thirty.

It is a delight to rest again in our own little corner here in this holy retreat, far from the haunts of passion and the marts of greed, where men are real brothers, and our gracious Father looks with lovingkindness upon us all.

Affectionately, your fellow disciple, '

Julian P. Johnson

Eight

A Christmas Meditation

The Dera
January 1, 1933

Beloved Friends in America,

Christmas morning on the banks of the Beas River in India, a solitary American sits in meditation. Tides of memories and emotions sweep over him. Far away in the homeland this morning millions gather about their firesides in joyful reunion to celebrate the birth of a baby nineteen and a third centuries ago. Why do they do it? And why is this American so far from his home this morning here in a strange land? Who can penetrate the veil and solve the mysteries that constitute the phenomena of human life? Only the Master.

Wise men set out for Bethlehem

Here we sit by the slow-rolling waters of an Indian river. India, the changeless India, the eternal mother. From her mountains and plains almost two thousand years ago went three wise men, Masters, setting out on the long overland journey to an obscure village in a remote province of a Roman Empire. An event was about to transpire to which they alone had full knowledge. Over long and weary stretches of desert, of vale and mountain roads, the camels beat their steady tread westward. Guided by the inner light, whose star burned

92

brighter as they approached their destination, the wise men came at last to a little Essene inn, dug into the hillside in Bethlehem. The Masters know the significance of all events. That is one reason they are called wise men. They know the value, also the past and the future of every soul coming into the world. As these wise men halted in the silent watches of the night on the plains of Bethlehem and looked down upon the little Judean village composed mostly of shepherds and farmers, they knew that an illuminated soul was about to take human birth there, and their gladness and immeasurable love drew down from heaven a great chorus who startled the sleepy shepherds with their holy song. Thus heralded, came the Son of Mary. And now after the lapse of centuries, the sweet story is told in awed whispers about the Christmas firesides. And the holy melody lingers in the hearts of men.

A gloomy Christmas day

But this disciple sits alone on the banks of the river far from his native land, and about him there is no Christmas celebration. The day itself is dreary. Clouds overhang the sky and chill winds blow. The dear Master of the Dera is in Agra today, and only the persian wheel at the well goes on forever as it has done for ages. Even Paras Ram, the servant boy, usually so good, is in an ugly mood today because he could not have his own way this morning. Christmas morning on the banks of the Beas. Here there will be no turkey dinner today. No Christmas frolic tonight. No gathering of the kiddies to inspect armloads of toys. Far away in her California home is a little one, "so mighty like a rose" in the sweet bloom of her childhood, so beautiful that it seems as if she had just stepped down out of paradise bringing the light of that world with her. Perhaps with dawning intuition she sits today, waits and wonders. May the holy angels guard her "all through the night."

A tear drops by the river

And there by the banks of the Beas River a lone student sits and wonders. But the unheeding river flows on as it has done for half a million years and more. What cares it for Christmas babies? What cares it for saints and holy shrines? What cares it for a hundred million souls ground down beneath the Wheel? Only time, time and worked out karma, and the love of God, shall bring release. This far wanderer may be excused if he drops a silent tear today upon the banks of the unheeding river. Yet why the tear? It would be hard to say. Does he wish today that he was back in America? No, a thousand times no. His emotions may be partly from thoughts of loved ones so far away, partly from pity for those who, like himself, have stumbled so long through the darkness; and partly for pure joy, joy that he at last has found the way to the light. Fifty years of searching up and down the earth, restless, drifting, listening, hoping vaguely for—he knew not what. But at last the Master who knows and loves took his hand, like a gracious father, and led him out of the wilderness. Over land and sea he almost dragged the wanderer, until at last he rested at the holy feet of his redeemer.

And strangely enough, that redeemer in his human form dwells here on the banks of the Beas River. The light of this stupendous truth is dazzling to the eyes of perception. How can it be so? Yet the pure white music of it, the living joy of it, fills the soul of the wanderer as he sits today upon the banks of the unheeding river. When the world seemed but a prisonhouse of confusion and pain, the blessed Master came across the seas and touched my soul. He came to give freedom. He came in the stillness of the night, while I watched and prayed. Suddenly he came, and the light of a thousand suns shone about him, though my dull eyes could not see the glory of the light. He called me, and my soul heard the divine music of his voice. No fetters of earth can hold me now. They all drop away like wax melting in white fires. He bade me come to him on the banks of the Beas where he could teach me the wisdom of the holy path; teach me and train me and watch over me as a father, feed me on the bread of life and help me to grow clean and strong and fearless, fit at last to stand before the radiant Lord. No more wandering in strange by-paths. No more groping in the wilderness, but a steady climbing with him up to the heights. And when the awakened soul at last touches the pure white sea, this divine drop, grown all luminous itself, shall be absorbed in that shining sea.

And so, after all, this Christmas morning may mean more to the lone American on the banks of the Beas than it does to millions of other Americans at their turkey dinners in the homeland.

Jesus and the Jews
But happy as this disciple is today at the feet of a living Master, he can never forget, nor fail to appreciate the dear Son of Mary, even though the story of his life comes down to us dimmed by the intervening centuries. Like that of all spiritual Masters, his life was a sweet mystery, and its main value to us now is the love it brought into the world. In that long ago, Jesus came to the Jews as a light to guide their erring feet. They sadly needed him. For a long time fancying themselves the specially chosen people of God, yet falling into diverse errors and sins, now ascendant and now subject, they at last pitifully sat and nursed their woes under the galling yoke of Rome. But they fondly imagined that their Jehovah would come someday to their rescue and restore to them not only their freedom, but give to them world dominion. Thus they

waited for the coming messiah. While they fondled this egotistical dream, the great teacher came and they failed to recognize him. He came as a light to both Jews and Gentiles,
and they both joined in crucifying him.

Being full of enmity toward each other, nothing in the
world could have induced the Jews and Gentiles to join hands
in any constructive activity for the good of mankind; but they
readily joined in the murder of the best man in all the Roman
Empire. Such is the venomous quality of religious prejudice.

His own great heart strained with grief as he stood upon
Mount Olivet and looked upon the city of David. Knowing
their many weaknesses and being full of pity, he exclaimed,
"Oh, Jerusalem, Jerusalem, how oft would I have gathered
thy children together as a hen gathers her chickens under her
wings, and ye would not."

Jesus himself was born to Jewish parents, his father being
a member of the Essene Brotherhood. He inherited the restless mind, the fiery impulse and the passionate love of the
Semite, as well as spiritual insight and lofty idealism. To this
heritage he added the training in scientific yoga of Mother
India. (For he spent some time in India.) Returning from
India, fired by an amazing love, he came to his own people
like the flash of a meteor. He taught them and healed their
diseases in vast multitudes, and then he passed to higher regions, leaving them dazzled at his light, but not comprehend-
ing it. So it has always been. Only those who know his inner
life love him, and to them even to this day his memory is like
the odor of sweet incense. He is worthy of all the love that
Christmas can bring him.

But one thing the American people have not yet learned,
which is vastly more important than the memories of all past
ages. That is the fact that more than one Christ has come
into the world and some of them are still in the body carry-

ing on their great work. The same need and the same divine
love that brought one, has brought a long succession of them.
The same great Father who sent one noble son to Bethlehem
has sent a great number of them to many lands and in many
ages. In fact the world is never without at least one of them.

Other Christs are born

Only a few days ago this disciple visited the birthplace of another of these great souls, the world's lightbearers and redeemers. In a little village called Ghoman, in Punjab, was born in
the year 1839 a child endowed with spiritual possibilities of a
transcendent character. In the humble quarters of a family of
farmers in this little village Baba Jaimal Singh was born. No
angel chorus announced his coming and yet he was born to a
destiny among the greatest of the sons of men. He became a
disciple of the great Soami Ji, and later rose to real sainthood
himself. He laid the foundations of this work in Punjab.

While the star of that Saint burned brightly in the Indian
sky, another star of the first magnitude arose over "the land
of five waters."* In 1858 another babe was born here who has
become another Christ, and whose holy mission has already
engirdled the earth itself with streams of light. It is he at whose
holy feet this disciple is now permitted to sit. His very name,
Sawan, meaning showers, points to the character of his work.
As the summer rains bring new life to the dry land, so this
great Saint showers the water of life upon all who come to
him. Other saviors also have come and gone, in India and in
other lands. They came and their lights burned with intense
brilliancy for a time and then disappeared. For this dark planet
was not their home. But the perfume of their holy lives has
lingered like the odor of sweet incense, like frankincense and

---

* Literally, the word *Punjab* means "five waters."

myrrh. Many a soul, long ages under the Wheel, found release by the strong hand of these Masters, and vast numbers
more would have escaped if only they had heeded the voice
of these redeemers. If this disciple ever spends Christmas in
America again, he will surely spend it, not in eating a big turkey dinner, but in trying to show his people that they may
have access to a living Christ, abiding yet in the body and
abundantly able to save unto the uttermost all who seek shelter at his holy feet.

Sitting at his feet

Some days ago this disciple sat at the feet of the beloved Master on the very edge of the bank of this unheeding river. He
had gone there to see to the unloading of three barges full of
reeds for use in the Dera. The bringing of these reeds was
purely a labor of love, no one receiving any cash pay; and yet
scores of men, and even some women, engaged in the work
eagerly. The reeds were carried in bundles on their heads up
the slopes to the Dera, from the steep river banks. The Master sat in a chair and this disciple sat on the ground at his
feet. To sit there was better than to sit in royal chairs. Through
all of India, and to the ends of the earth, there is no place so
sacred as at the feet of a living saint. He who is privileged to
sit there is blessed above all others. To look into the eyes of
divine love, to listen to his voice full of the resonance of the
highest spiritual culture, to feel in the depths of one's own
soul the warm glow of his holy light—that is something never
to be forgotten when once experienced. How precious the
moments. After a pilgrimage through the long and weary
years, life after life, slowly emerging from the slime and the
darkness of sin and ignorance, at last to sit at the feet of a
living saint, and to know that never again shall the soul de-

scend into the depths, but shall mount with the Master up to the regions of light. This is a joy that no Christmas dinner can give, and for this holy hour one may well travel all the highways of earth and sail the seven seas.

Illustrating the extreme value of the privilege described above, a story is told of Lord Shiva. It is said that while walking through the jungle one day, he came upon a certain spot and, stopping, began to weep. When asked why he wept, he said, "Ten thousand years ago a true saint sat down upon this sacred spot and I was not here to see him and worship at his holy feet."

Now after seven months with this dear Master, the American disciple feels that even the disciple himself no longer exists as a separate individual. Besides the Master, there is no one else. There is nothing. The Master is all there is.

Sunset and moonrise on the Beas

We began the day on the banks of the Beas River. Let us end it there. But the scene has changed. The cheerless gray of the morning has given place to a great burst of light from out of a gorgeously painted sky. The moon also has just risen. Stand here by me on the banks of this unheeding river for a few minutes and let me show you a most beautiful sight. For after all, the river is kind in spite of its apparent indifference to our emotions.

Everyone here feels that at all times the Dera is a sacred spot. It has been so from the time that Baba Jaimal Singh, that beloved Saint who was Guru to our own Master, first hung his string of dry loaves of bread upon a tree and sat down to meditate by the banks of this river. Day and night he sat, and when hunger impelled him he would soften a portion of a loaf in water and eat it, returning at once to his devotions. It is said here that this great Master foresaw this as a splendid center of spiritual activity, extending its influence to the ends of the earth. At that time, forty-one years ago, there was but little here except vast wastes of land and unwatered silt. Now, irrigated green fields make the whole countryside like a garden. This beautiful little Dera, now rapidly growing to be a real town, becomes more and more the sixty-ninth place of public pilgrimage in India. This is due to the life and work of our own great Master. In addition to its sacred associations, the place has its natural attractions, not the least among which are its river and its beautiful sunsets.

The Dera in sunset glory

Just now the sun is lowering his brilliant disc behind the buildings of the Dera. Orange and deep red and purple light up the western sky. And those gorgeous colors, somewhat softened in tone, are reflected in the river. Tones and shades of colors are rapidly changing in both sky and river. Like a silver band a quarter of a mile wide, the river stretches away to the south, visible for two or three miles, also winding its way into the north, visible for eight or ten miles in that direction. The west bank on which we stand rises from fifty to a hundred feet above water and is cut by many deep ravines where the rains, during millennia of time, have washed the soil into the river. On the banks of a ravine some three hundred yards away sit two *sadhus* (ascetics) in meditation. No, at this moment they are chanting a sacred hymn. On the north side of the Dera can be heard the incessant click of the persian wheel as it brings up water from a sixty-foot well, to the slow and monotonous tread of the oxen. Across the river to the east, long levels of yellow sandbars are streaked with patches of dark brown earth. Beyond them are faintly visible numerous fields of yellow and gray in the gathering shadows. And far away in the east a greenish-gray line of trees meets the deep blue sky. Hung in that deep blue sky is the clear full moon, now a half-hour above the horizon. Its silvery face is reflected in the river by a long path of white and sparkling ripples, so gentle that their motion is barely perceptible. The flow of the river is slow, so it rolls along with just enough movement to break the glassy smoothness of its deep and silent waters.

The violet in the sky is now reflected from the river, forming a most unique border to the silver sheen of the reflected moon. The western sky gradually changes to pale gold, while to the south the orange merges into red and purple, and that into deep blue and steel gray. The light fades rapidly. The glistening waters of the river in the north now stand out above the yellow sands leaving them but a faint blur. The timber line on the eastern horizon has become a black border against the steel gray of the sky. Now the last sandbar disappears. Only the river and the moon and the shadowy earth remain, and the silence of the night.

Finally the buildings of the Dera are sharply outlined against the western sky. The eye of the observer searches for one bright electric light that usually shines at night, like a mariner's beacon, above the Master's house. But tonight that light is absent. The Master is not there. Only the light of his love and goodness remains with us. At last only a silvery streak marks the waters of the Beas River, merging into its black shorelines. The pale afterglow of sunset tells us that another day has passed. Mounting the eastern sky, the queen of the night is now supreme.

This disciple then asked the "man in the moon" if he had any message from his country and people so far away on the opposite side of the earth, but the "man in the moon" replied, with a twinkle in his eye, "Never mind your country and people; it is time you were getting back to your *bhajan*."

So, we must bid you goodnight, and
"God be with you till we meet again."

Your loving fellow disciple,

Julian P. Johnson

Nine

Beloved American Satsangis,

In this letter I want to give you first a few hints regarding some of the difficulties experienced by a newcomer in India. You shall then have something better in the last section of the letter.

A combination salad in Calcutta

On board ship the writer made the acquaintance of a very affable and cultured Hindu gentleman who was of great assistance to him during the six hours he spent in Calcutta. After many weeks aboard ship, saturated with unsavory smells, and finally free upon solid ground once more, one feels that a good square meal would be about the most desirable thing imaginable. So we set off to find a restaurant where they served vegetable curry and rice. We heard of such a place. After walking sixteen and two-thirds blocks, we found the place, only to be told that they were just out, no more prepared just now. But they told us of another place. Walking nine and a half blocks more—walking is good for one after a long sea voyage—we were told sadly that they never made strictly vegetable curry. Why should anyone want vegetable curry, least of all an American *sahib?* They would serve a choice chicken curry immediately for one rupee and a half. But we asked for a vegetable combination salad. Yes, yes, they would serve it at once. Will the sahib please be seated.

After waiting about half an hour, a boy entered with a basket full of vegetables and passed to a back room. Fifteen minutes later the proprietor entered the dining room, triumphantly carrying a broad smile and the combination salad. It consisted of three pieces of green peppers, one and a half slices of tomato, two pieces of onion and nine shreds of cabbage topped off with a small pod of red pepper, just to give it artistic effect. Asked for a salad dressing the proprietor looked pained and disappointed. His salad was not duly appreciated. These Americans are such unreasonable creatures, anyway. They are all so rich and live in such unbounded luxury that they are badly spoiled. Why should anyone wish anything else on a fine salad like that? Wasn't the red pepper sufficient for relish? My educated friend explained in the vernacular, and so after serious conferences with the elders of the establishment, and much grave discussion, it was finally agreed that if the sahib wished, they would send out and get some olive oil. The sahib did not care.

Railway travel in India

Going to the depot—they always say station in this country—to take a train, one has to decide first of all what sort of a person he is—whether first class, second class, intermediate, or altogether third rate. If he thinks he is first class and wishes to travel that way, he pays a rate a little higher than the regular railroad fare in America. But in this country it is much the same as in England, where they have a saying that only lords, Americans and fools travel first class. If one decides that he is second class, or his purse is second class, he pays only about half of the first class rate. The intermediate is about one half of the second class rate, and the third class is much cheaper still.

Let us suppose that he elects to travel intermediate. He will get there just as soon as if he traveled first class. He looks about for a window where they sell that class of tickets. Getting his ticket, he then enters his compartment on the side, directly from the platform. He has access only to his own compartment, which consists of two, four, or six benches. The backs of the benches are absolutely straight up and down, even in the first and second classes. After sitting on one for twenty-four hours, one is quite certain that if they could have made them more uncomfortable, they surely would have done so. The first and second-class compartments have electric fans and cushions on the backs and bottoms of the benches. The intermediate has only wooden benches with a very poor sort of cushion, and the third class is but little better than an American box car with just wooden benches to sit on. The only cheerful thing about them is the fact that they will take you to your destination.

Entering your intermediate compartment, it dawns upon you for the first time in the confusion of many strange things, that you will really have to spend the night on the train, and where are you going to sleep? There are no Pullman coaches; not even tourist sleepers. And this is a fast transcontinental mail train, the best in India. If your friends have not properly informed you to carry your own bedding with you, you are just out of luck. But if you have your own roll of bedding, you spread it out on the hard wooden bench, with its suggestion of a cushion, and proceed to make yourself as comfortable as circumstances will permit. It is always equivalent to many riches, if you learn to be satisfied with whatever your lot may be.

You ride along for an hour and a half, wondering what the country outside is like, while the dust and hot winds sift about the compartment. You begin to feel sleepy and settle down for a nap. The train comes to a grinding stop. Loud voices rend the sultry night air. If there is any one thing in India that is more obtrusive than another, it is loud talking. It is the only thing they ever do in a hurry. Let two or three of the coolie, or laboring class, get a little excited or angry, and the speed at which their mouths discharge noises is something that even Einstein never dreamed of. The velocity of light is a slow pace. It sounds as if ten thousand words to the minute would be a conservative estimate. But of course no one has ever been able to count the words, and so the speed limit is not known. It is amazing how any human machine can work so fast and emit such volumes of sound. Certainly no one can understand half of what is said; neither is it important, or even desirable, that any should understand. It is simply an automatic explosion of the agitated ego.

But we must return to our train. Loud voices on the platform. Mobs of people, vendors of soda water, fruits and sweet meats, cry their wares. Your compartment is already full; but in India there are three hundred and fifty million people. Now the door opens and five fat men and three boys tumble in, carrying sixteen bundles of assorted sizes, ranging all the way from a jug of water to a chicken coop, filled with fancy hens, or it may be a litter of pups. They—the men and pups—look about. No room to sit down. Bundles are piled on the floor and the boys climb on top of them. The men fix their eyes on you, lying stretched out on that bench. It is a sad case, but you simply have to get up. You have not paid for the entire bench. You roll up your bedding and sit upon it, leaning against the perpendicular wall. When morning comes, as it always does come, thank heaven, even in Indian railway cars, you are still sitting on your roll, leaning against the perpendicular wall. The fat men and boys are scattered here and there, over benches and bundles, crumpled up, nodding and snoring. The old men are chattering at each other, no one listening, while the train rumbles on through the dust and sultry winds.

The food question

Of course, the food question is a pressing one from the beginning. Man usually has the foolish notion that he must eat, every day or two, at least. He looks for a restaurant. He watches for familiar windows with a display of appetizing foods. No sign of them in India. What is to be done? He soon learns that he should have carried his own food with him, as well as his bedding, soap and towels. However, he can get meals on the big through trains if he is willing to eat them and pay the price. He can get lunches also at some of the principal stations. But for a strict vegetarian it is often a rather difficult problem.

Comfortably settled at last at the end of his journey and a faithful servant urging him to eat, the American is again quite satisfied. The boy enters with a full tray; little copper dishes each filled with something, the like of which he never looked upon before, and on a large copper platter a stack of something that resembles pancakes. You lift one. It feels hard and heavy. It is a *chapatti*, the standard bread here, made of whole wheat flour, salt and water, and baked on a piece of sheet iron. In the Dera they bake them by the thousand per hour when big crowds gather. In each copper dish a native vegetable, literally swimming in grease, which they call *ghee*. In India ghee is much loved, and if they wish to be especially nice to a guest, they simply add a little more ghee to his food. Besides the ghee, each vegetable is seasoned with two to six different spices of assorted flavors and odors wholly unlike anything you ever tasted or smelled before. One of the greatest difficulties encountered by this writer has been to keep his servant from putting all the 57 varieties of seasoning spices into his food. Without them he thinks the food would be tasteless.

The song of the mosquito

The date is June 14. Real summer in Punjab. The two small boys appointed to pull the *punka** to keep the air in motion in the room have grown tired of their monotonous job, and one of them is stretched out on the floor, sound asleep. The other one is so sleepy that his hand relaxes the rope, the punka slows down to a complete stop, and he leans back against the wall, asleep. Presently beads of perspiration stand out all over you. The temperature is 120° F in your room. Paras Ram, the servant boy, enters the room for the twenty-seventh time in two hours to ask if the sahib will have another glass of lemon soda, which he calls lemonade. This drink is quite a welcome refreshment during the hot weather in India. When night falls the newcomer seeks relief from the oppressive heat of the rooms below by going up to the roof. Here he is greeted by the silvery moon, just risen above the valley of the Beas River. As soon as he can get rid of an overanxious servant, he lies down on his cot to rest and listen to the chanting of fifty women, in the Dera kitchen, as they sing in unison their song of devotion to Satguru, while they cook chapattis. The howl of jackals in the distant jungle and the persistent song of a quartette of mosquitoes keep him company as he slips away into dreamland.

---

* *Punka*, a large cloth fan suspended from the ceiling and kept in constant motion by pulling ropes.

Talk less, eat less, sleep less

In the morning your servant awakens you when he thinks you have slept too long. He coughs a little louder than usual, or rattles a dish. It is not good for you to sleep so late, especially after your tea is poured, piping hot. Your servant knows what is best for you, and above all he knows what is *tik* or proper. The very day this writer arrived here, a bright satsangi informed him that as one advances in this Path, he eats less, sleeps less and talks less. Your servant will see to it that you sleep less. With a little encouragement, he will volunteer to do most of the talking for you; but if you should eat all he sets before you, you would not survive a single month. In spite of pleadings and scoldings, he continues to serve enough for five men.

Once you are seated at your breakfast table, your servant places before you a pot of tea and two small biscuits—little sweet crackers. You prefer coffee, but he sadly informs you that there is no coffee in town. Besides it is quite incredible that anyone should prefer coffee to tea. Does not every English gentleman in the world drink tea precisely at six o'clock every morning? You surrender and reach for the tea, but the servant jumps for the pot and pours the tea himself. It is not *tik* that a sahib should pour his own tea. You look for the cream. At least you might have cream in your tea, if you cannot have coffee. But he passes you a cup of milk, boiled and sweetened. Anyway, it is very strange that a man should want cream in his tea. One should use only sugar in tea. But these Americans have such peculiar notions.

Months after this American was settled here in his own little corner, he was able to get a man to bring milk to his own rooms, so that he could let it stand overnight and have cream for his coffee the next morning; also to avoid having the milk boiled and sweetened, which is the universal custom here. So the next morning he looked forward to enjoying real cream in his coffee for the first time since leaving America. But when the coffee was served, a jug of milk was set before him. Asked about the cream, the servant exhibited a pained and blank expression. He had carefully stirred the cream and milk together again, thinking it would surely be much better that way. It was quite incredible that anyone should want pure cream in his coffee, when he might have milk and cream both together.

Hands made before towels

One day, following a severe dust storm, a plate was put on the table quite covered with dust. It was handed to the servant to be cleaned. He took it in the most casual manner and proceeded to wipe the dust off with his bare hands. One day, after sending away to a distant city for baking powder, the writer proceeded to make wholewheat pancakes, à la americaine. Charcoal was placed in a little iron box and a plate of steel was set over the hot coals. Ghee was poured over the steel plate and the batter was spread. The pancakes were nicely browned at last. The servant looked on with eager snapping eyes, picked up the extra plate off the floor, wiped off the dust with his bare hands, and then picked up the hot pancakes, one at a time, in his fingers, and put them on the plate. When told that he must handle them with a knife or fork—no pancake turners known—he was amazed that anyone should prefer clumsy instruments to his own hands, even for handling hot pancakes.

There is no such thing as fresh butter in this country, except in a few of the larger cities that have modern dairies, or where people are especially taught to make it. What they use for butter is extracted from milk after a long process of boiling and mixing and separating. The taste and the odor are both rather difficult for an American to surmount.

Beds and feather pillows unknown

There are no such things as bedsprings and mattresses. Your beds consist of a roll of blankets spread upon cots made by stretching ropes or strips of canvas over wooden frames which stand up on four legs a foot or more from the ground. Then your pillows—you pick them up and try to diagnose them. After a night spent on one, you still wonder. Certainly not feathers. They are made of cotton, fiber, wood, or bricks; one cannot say exactly which. The writer tried in the great city of Lahore to purchase a feather pillow. He went to a shop. No big department stores. Only shops, each specializing in certain articles. He asked for pillows. Yes, yes, plenty of pillows. They always say yes in this country, no matter what your question may be. Say to a man, "How are you this morning?" and he will say, "Yes, thank you." It is considered polite to say yes first. But his pillows were all of the hard variety. Asked for feather pillows, he said, "Yes, yes," and turned and asked another man, he a third, and he a fourth. Finally, the answer came back that they had no such pillows. Another shop was tried with the same results. Then a third shop. Finally it became apparent that they had no idea of what was meant by feather pillows. When asked if they had any feather pillows in India, the shopkeeper said, "Yes, yes," turned and asked another man, he a third one, and he a fourth, then all of the bystanders were consulted. At last the answer came back that they did not understand what the sahib meant. The sahib then tried to explain that feather pillows were made by pulling feathers out of a duck or goose, or other fowls, sewing them into bags, and using them for pillows. The shopkeepers and bystanders listened with growing incredulity, with half-suspicious expressions on their faces, and glances from one to another, as if they suspected that the foreign sahib was actually exhibiting signs of insanity.

A land of many languages

Of course the language is one of the big difficulties, and the problem is doubly difficult here because it is a country of many languages. It is said that more than three hundred different languages and dialects are spoken in India. The writer started out to study Hindi. He applied himself diligently for a time, making some headway. He would work out a few sentences with much pains and labor—one might almost say, with labor pains. Then he would start out with malicious intent to use them on the first innocent person he ran across. Finally cornering someone, with deliberate aim he would discharge his sentences at the unsuspecting victim. If he was unable to speak English, he simply looked puzzled, perhaps smiled a little, and passed on. If he could understand a little English, he would ask, "What did you say, sir?" The Hindi sentences are repeated. He knots his brow and asks again, "I did not understand, sir. What did you say?" Then all crestfallen, the American repeats in English what he thought he was saying in Hindi. The kindhearted person then smiles sympathetically and asks to have the Hindi sentences repeated once more. It is done with great care and painstaking effort, with strict regard for grammatical precision. The face of the person lights up. He has understood. At last you have triumphed. But the person adds, "Yes, yes, that is quite all right; perfectly correct, sir—only that is not the way we say it." He is then asked to say it right, and he says something which sounds not at all like anything the American had ever heard before.

Urdu, Hindi, and Punjabi are all spoken here. Punjabi is sometimes called Gurmukhi. Asked to explain the difference between these three languages, the average person will tell you in substance, "No difference at all; they are exactly the same, only different." They will then tell you how Hindi is made up more of pure Sanskrit, Urdu being a mixture of Hindi, Persian, Arabic and Sanskrit, while Punjabi is a mixture of them all. Punjabi is to some extent a manufactured language, having been modified by one of the Sikh Gurus, and so it is considered almost a sacred tongue by the Sikhs. It is the language in which their sacred book is written.

The problem of traffic congestion

If you are traveling on the highways or city streets of this country, the problem of traffic congestion is always present. In the main streets and on the sidewalks of Calcutta you may have to push the cows out of your way to get by. If you are in a motorcar on almost any highway, you are confronted by a mob of people, and filling in all of the spaces between the people are various assortments of cows, oxcarts, camels, buffaloes, calves, donkeys, dogs, and sometimes geese, ducks, and chickens. The horn is sounded nearly all of the time, but no one pays any attention to it until the car is right on them, and then they jump, sometimes in the right direction. When the writer was in India on his first trip, forty-two years ago, he was riding a bicycle one day down a broad and beautiful boulevard in Bangalore City. A crowd of people strolled along in front of him in the center of the street. The alarm bell was rung and rung, but no one heeded the bell. Finally he turned to go around a bunch of men who were directly in front of him; just at that moment a man jumped, of course, in the wrong direction, right in front of the wheel. There was a bump in the rear, which probably left a bump in the same region. A general scatterment. Much loud talking by the crowd, while the two of us sat in the midst of the street and looked at each other—looked and wondered.

And so one might go on for hours, recounting the minor difficulties one encounters as a stranger in this country. But to a serious student, here to follow the Master, those things are, as they say here, *kuchh nahin*, "nothing at all." Although this letter is already long enough, we cannot close it without some reference to the Master. So let us make the closing section consist of something more interesting and important.

A parable of the ballroom

The dance is in full swing. Costly gowns and sparkling jewels, bare white skin, powder and rouge, light and music and wine, beauty and laughter and love, all mingle in one gorgeous night. During a pause in the music, a couple slip away into the garden. What a night! The moon and the stars were never so bright, and the perfume of a myriad flowers saturates the night air. A night just made for lovers and loving. They pass on into secluded byways. And all the while, five deadly foes walk on either side of them and behind them. But their footsteps are not heard and their hideous aspects are not seen. The wine has flushed the cheeks of our happy couple and emboldened their desires. The world is now shut out. They hold each other in close embrace and murmur endearing words. Of all sweet things on earth, she is the most charming. Of all men in the world, he is the one just made for her alone. Nothing shall ever again separate them. Though all others have had troubles, they will never have any. Life shall be one long happy song of love. So they hold each other closer and press each other's lips in a long, delicious, intoxicating kiss. And the five deadly foes, all unseen by them, smile at each other, as they nod their approval.

The lovers are utterly lost to the world. They have each other. Nothing else counts. And they have life, real life. Away with your narrow creeds of self-control and the laws of karma. They are all right for old women, but for red-blooded youth they are "bunk." Youth must live. Enjoy the present. The individual ego must express itself. Besides, we live only once and then—who knows what? Let wine and love chase away the shadows of the night and banish dull care and old men's superstitions. We must know life as it is. Let the future take care of itself. Tonight we shall drink and love. So, time and space and God, and the laws of karma, are all forgotten in a whirl of blissful frenzy, intoxication of passion. And while they float away in the ecstasy of sweet delirium, the five deadly foes creep up and each one injects into the veins of the dreamers his own particular kind of poison. Some inner sense of danger causes them a little uneasiness, but the resistless tide of passion sweeps them on. They will enjoy the moment, let come what may. The poison enters their bodies and permeates even to the bones.

Only leaves, dead leaves

Time passes. It may be a day or a year, or forty years. But it passes, and the gray dawn breaks at last. The sleeper stirs and mutters some half-forgotten words of endearment and extends his arms. But they close on empty space. His beloved is not there. He sits up somewhat startled. He feels a dull pain in his head and limbs. His throat is dry. He feels about him and his hands grasp a large bundle of papers. He looks. Only bills, bills, bills; and at the foot of each one are written the ominous words, "Please remit." The words burn themselves into his brain. In the sweet delirium of his pleasures, he had forgotten that he must pay. He feels about for his purse, once bulging with banknotes. But now it is gone. He reaches again. His hands grasp something. Only leaves, dead leaves, cold and damp in the fogs of the night air— leaves of faded hopes and burned-out passions. Only a handful of dead leaves, and on each leaf are written the ominous words, "Please remit."

Only dead leaves now, and the cold damp earth. Nothing

more. He looks at his hand. He feels his face. The skin is rough and wrinkled. His hair is quite gray. The five poisons have done their deadly work. He is now an old man, full of disease and pain. What could have happened to him? Only a few hours ago, he was young and full of joy and the sweet intoxication of love. He never expected anything like this. And where was his beloved? Why wasn't she at his side? He struggled to his feet and walked on through the dismal woods that had so recently been a garden of exquisite beauty, full of roses and lilacs, sweet hyacinths and violets. But now even the trees were bare and the chill autumn winds whistled through the dead limbs. Presently he stumbled over something and fell to his knees. Peering with amazement at the form before him, he exclaimed, "Mary, for God's sake, what has happened?" But a harsh and accusing voice replied, "Aye, and what is the matter with you?" Still gazing into the gaunt and haggard face before him he thought, "Great God, is that the thing I loved but an hour ago?" Then out of the depths of anguish and bitter disappointment, he cried aloud, "My God, my God, what is it all about?" Still looking anxiously at the "thing" on the ground, he muttered, "Water, water!" And then as he reached for the empty cup, his hand dropped, his chin rested on his chest, and the body pitched forward to the ground. Another soul had passed under the Wheel.

Master enters the dance hall

Going back to the dance hall, let us follow another scene for a few minutes. In the midst of the gay whirl, an elderly man enters. He wears a tall white turban, East Indian fashion, a long light-colored coat, raja style, light trousers and tan-colored oxfords. He has a long white beard. His bearing is noble, as that of a born king, and his countenance is like the rays of the morning sun. His voice is low and musical and full of tenderness. He spreads about him an atmosphere of holy peace. Even the dance hall seems sacred in his presence. But for the most part, he excites only a mild curiosity and a casual remark or two. One half-intoxicated woman, leaning on the chest of her escort, said, "Who is the old beard? Wouldn't it be fun if you had one like that!" The mad whirl of the dance goes on uninterrupted. The wine flows as before. And the five deadly foes stalk through the crowd unnoticed, except by the sharp eyes of the newcomer.

But one lone couple, sitting apart from the crowd, apparently in deep thought, took special notice of the stranger. They arose and hastened to meet him, a new light beaming in their eyes. With a smile he greeted them, and led them away from the crowd to a flight of stairs leading to an upper room which was wholly unknown to most of the guests. Entering this room, the couple fell down and worshipped him; for now they knew that he was the Master. As soon as they had reached that upper room, they noticed that his form had changed. It had become all radiant and beautiful beyond the power of words to describe, and each ray of light streaming from it, white and golden in color, seemed to carry a stream of divine melody which was in itself the very essence of life, truth and wisdom and love. They worshipped him with trembling and great joy—a joy the world never can know. Taking their hands, he bade them rise and look behind them. Much to their amazement, they saw that they had not entered the room alone, but close behind each of them had come five others whose aspects were extremely uninviting. They were the five deadly enemies of mankind: *kam* (passion), *krodh* (anger), *lobh* (greed), *moh* (attachment), and *ahankar* (egotism or vanity). These five cowered in much fear at the sight of the Master and would have fled, but they could not detach themselves from those they followed, being held by many fine, strong, but invisible threads, threads that had required ages to weave.

N-A-M, *the sword*

The Master now presented to each of the couple a most beautiful sword, a sword of the finest steel, finer than the finest blade of Damascus. And the sword was so constructed that if one listened carefully, he could hear, emanating from it, the sweetest strains of music. On the golden hilt of each sword was engraved in shining white, the letters: N-A-M. The Master bade them take this sword and returning below among the common walks of men, proceed to give battle to those five deadly enemies. They obeyed his commands at once and right gladly. They fought, and long was the fight, sometimes discouraging, but always they fought on with increasing determination. The radiant form of the Master never left them for a moment, always giving courage and strength. With every steady thrust of the sword they grew stronger, while their enemies grew weaker. At last the battle was over, the victory won. While the struggling souls fought their way against the five deadly agents of the negative power, they were steadily advancing to higher ground. When at last their victory was complete, they stood upon the heights of dazzling splendor upon the plains of Daswan Dwar. The Master's approval was their greatest joy, but their journey was not yet finished. So they followed the Master onward and upward, pursuing their glorious way with increasing joy, until they rested at last before the all-luminous feet of the supreme Lord. They had entered the realm of immortal life, and of immeasurable happiness.

With greetings of love and best wishes
From your fellow disciple,

Julian P. Johnson

Ten

Dear Fellow Students,

I have been asked by some of you for my opinion on the much discussed subject of *swaraj,* home rule, or the problem of the British rule in India. The question of the British Raj in India, which is now agitating the public mind especially on account of the part played by Mahatma Gandhi, is not a question to be settled by a foreigner. That would be equivalent to the old maid teaching parents how to raise children. It is a profound and complicated problem. It is a question concerning which this writer is not well informed and in which he is but little interested. Consequently, he will not attempt to discuss it. But he might venture two statements, which may help the student in his study of the problem.

The problem of swaraj

First, the British rule in India has, in many ways, been a very great blessing to the country, and we believe it has been better for India, notwithstanding its faults, than any other existing government would have been. It has been set over India by the supreme will. Let us keep that in mind. Because all kings and governments exist only by His will. This writer only a few days ago asked a highly educated native gentleman the following question: "Don't your people like the British

119

government? They certainly have done much for India." And his reply was very significant. He said, "We like the British government all right, but we certainly do not like the machinery by which that government is administered." Here is a distinction not well understood by the world at large, and therein may lie the key to the final solution of the problem.

Second, out of the turmoil and stress of the present situation will arise a government best suited to enable India to regain something of her ancient prestige and then to go forward to achieve that sublime destiny now lying latent and germinal in the souls of her great spiritual leaders. Whether that government will be the one envisioned by Mahatma Gandhi and the Indian Congress, or a modified British Raj, is immaterial. Only one thing is certain—it will be the government best suited to serve the high destiny of this ancient and noble people. We may safely trust that to the supreme will, for His wisdom, inspired by an infinite love, never makes mistakes.

Since the above was first written and later published in an Indian magazine, the writer has received a letter from an Indian patriot, telling him that he would have done well to leave the subject alone, because India will be satisfied with nothing but independence. Let that be as it may. If the writer of that letter, and others who think the same way, had perfect faith in the supreme will, knowing that whatever He gives India will be the best thing for India, there would be but little grounds for further discussion.

The great Indian epic, Ramayana
In these letters I find myself far behind in making note of things I would like to tell you about. One of them is the festival of Diwali, which literally means the festival of lights. It occurred last year on October 29. It recalls the great Indian

epic, Ramayana, and celebrates the victorious return of Ram
Chandra after conquering and destroying his enemy, Ravan,
in Ceylon. The epic of Ramayana is one of the greatest ever
written. It is generally conceded to be far superior to either
the *Iliad* of Homer, or the *Divine Comedy* of Dante. It is
unique in one respect and for that reason I am referring to it
in these letters—it portrays the inner struggles of the soul
and its final victory over mind and matter. This it does in
well-adapted allegory. Its spiritual meaning was fully set forth
in writing by a saint named Tulsi Das about four hundred
years ago. But the original story was written in the Sanskrit
language so long ago that one cannot now venture to assign a
date to it—ages ago. One estimate is that it was written in
Treta Yuga, which would place it near two million years ago.
If this seems apocryphal to some of you, then have your own
way. The author of the original story was Balmiki, a great
sage or saint.

The epic is unique in one other respect—it was written at
least ten thousand years before its chief characters were born,
but who finally did appear and enacted their several parts in
actual history. For although this great epic is an exact por-
trayal of what takes place in each individual soul who struggles
to the light inside, yet the entire story was fully staged in history. The Master explains that the historical staging of the
great epic was an effort of the negative power to divert attention from its spiritual significance, and so make it appear to
all subsequent ages that the story is nothing more than a clever
poetical account of ordinary human exploits.

The story of Ram Chandra

Ram Chandra is the hero of the story, and his wife's name
was Sita. Ram Chandra was the eldest son of King Dashrath
and was heir to the throne of Kosala in northern India. The

major part of the story is woven around the abduction of Sita by Ravan, the evil-minded king of Lanka and the subsequent and consequent war between Ravan and Ram Chandra. Ram Chandra raised an army, many of them being monkeys, and invaded Lanka, attacking the vicious abductor of his beloved, and finally meeting him in single combat on the battlefield and slaying him. Thus he recovered his stolen wife who had remained true to him in spite of the advances and threats of her wicked abductor. To this day Sita is to all Indian women the model of virtue and faithfulness. The victorious return of Ram Chandra to the kingdom of his father was celebrated by lighting every light that could be produced, making the scene a most brilliant one. And so, down to the present time, all Hindus celebrate the anniversary of this great event by lighting all the lights that can be mustered for the occasion.

The spiritual meaning of Diwali

The spiritual significance of this festival of lights is the victorious entrance of the soul into Daswan Dwar after its final victory over mind and matter. The lights point to the splendor and beauty of that realm where even the light of one inhabitant is equal to the light of twelve of our suns.

I would like to go into details concerning some of the marvelous spiritual lessons pointed out to the student in this great epic of ancient India. But I cannot do so now. I have called attention to this perhaps the greatest classic ever produced by man, because it bears direct testimony in support of the teachings of our Master and other saints. The poem contains twenty-two thousand *slokas*, or couplets, and is divided into five hundred cantos. It is a pity that even now but few of the Indian people understand its true meaning, although they are so devoted to the story itself that every child in India is familiar with it. From the day that Ram Chandra, with almost superhuman strength and willpower, won his wife Sita (soul) in a public contest by bending and breaking the bow of Shiva (penetrating the darkness after controlling his own mind), up to his final victory, it is said that every word in every sentence is rich in spiritual meaning to him who has the key to its understanding.

I believe you may be able to get a very good translation of the Ramayana by applying to the state university, department of literature, for information.

Personnel of the Master's inner group

I desire now to give you a short sketch of the personnel of the Master's closest disciples and personal assistants. This will help you to follow the work of our great teacher. One cannot say that he has twelve disciples, for he has close to sixty thousand disciples, and most of them are devoted worshippers; but like all great men, he has a few who stand closest to him.

1. Naturally, we must begin with his private secretary, Rai Sahib, whose real name is Rai Harnarayan. He is always with the Master wherever he goes and is thus by his side to render assistance whenever and wherever needed. He is a retired director of public records in the Punjab civil government, and draws a liberal pension for long and meritorious services. Of course, he draws no salary for his present services, which are given purely from devotion to the Master and to the Master's work.

He is familiar with all of the languages spoken in this part of the country, including English. He is educated, highly efficient, and insists that things be done properly. One of his chief duties is to see that the Master is not imposed upon by everyone seeking selfish advantages. He has been an initiate of the Master for twenty-three years, and has been constantly with the Master for the past ten years. Evidently he is much loved by the Master and his services are greatly appreciated, not only by the Master but by all satsangis.

2. Next is Sardar Jagat Singh, professor of chemistry in the great agricultural college at Lyallpur. He is the secretary who attends to all of the American correspondence. All of the letters you get from the Master are in his handwriting, but the substance of those letters is dictated to him by the Master. He comes here as often as possible from a distance of 150 miles. If answers to some of your letters seem to be delayed at times, it is likely because he could not get time to attend to them. He is a mild-mannered man, gentle, of but few words, refined and deeply spiritual. In fact, he is a very lovable character. His devotion to the Master is an inspiration to all satsangis.

3. We may next introduce Sardar Bhagat Singh, a cousin of the professor, although in this country they speak of cousins as brothers. He is an attorney-at-law in Jullundur City, about 27 miles from here. (In this country an attorney registered to practice before the high court is called an advocate.) Sardar Bhagat Singh is one of the recognized outstanding men of his profession in all of Punjab. He is a man of medium height, rather heavy-set, with slightly gray beard and a benevolent smile that betokens a kind heart and a radiant soul. He is a lovable man and it is a delight to know him. He is highly educated, of a keen and discriminating intelligence, and he is a very successful lawyer. He is outstanding proof that a lawyer can make an honest living, for his honesty and integrity are beyond question. He attends to all of the legal work of the Master, relating to the many business affairs of this center. He may aptly be called the Prime Minister to the Master, a title which is commonly given him by satsangis.

4. Sardar Gajja Singh, a man of about forty-five or fifty years, is one of the advanced members of the Master's "cabinet".

He is a builder and architect. He is just now retiring from long service in the government and will be here shortly to assume charge of the construction work on the new auditorium to be built in the Dera, a picture of which appears in these pages. The bricks are now being burned here in the Master's own brick yard. Sardar Gajja Singh, or Baba Gajja Singh as he is affectionately known here, is renowned for his spiritual devotion and also for his love for the Master. He is highly trained and is a deep thinker in all matters philosophical and religious, as well as in his own particular profession. He draws plans and superintends all important construction work for the Master, although the Master himself is a civil engineer, and keeps his eye on everything that goes on.

5. Pritam Das fills an office not known in America. He is a chanter of sacred hymns and scriptures. At the satsangs a portion of the writings of some other saint, selected by the Master, is chanted by this man, usually assisted by one or two others. The Master then uses the portion chanted as his text. He makes comments and explanations. This takes the place of set lectures, in which the Master never indulges. This man used to be considered a Master himself and had many hundred disciples, although he is still less than forty years old. He had, and still has, the power to perform miracles and also the gift of prophecy. But of course he is now forbidden to use those powers. He was highly venerated. But he realized in his own soul that he had need for a perfect Master who could lead him to greater heights. Learning of our Master, he came to see him, was convinced of our Master's superiority over himself and all others, and asked for initiation. He then brought all of his own disciples to our Master, informing them of the Master's great superiority over himself.

6. Perhaps here we should introduce a man who, though not so highly educated or prominent in the social ranks, yet

occupies a position which, if rightly understood, might be envied even by the king-emperor. I am sure he would not exchange his present job for the crown of Great Britain. He has been the Master's personal attendant for the last seventeen years. He loves the Master with a devotion which is beautiful to see, and which only a true disciple can understand. He is over forty years of age and has never been married. He has always insisted that he cared for none other in this world except his Master. His name is Shadi, which means happiness. His sweet spirit is proverbial here. He is also a skilled mechanic and machinist. He is the silent watcher, as well as worshipper of his Master, ready at any moment of the day or night to render any service needed. That service, rewarded only by a smile or a kind word from the Master, is his greatest joy. Like all the rest, he gets no salary.

7. There are three women, Bibi Lajjo, Bibi Rakhi, and Bibi Rali, who render great service to the Master by preparing his food, doing his laundry, pressing his clothes, and doing his sewing, mending, etc. (Bibi is a sort of affectionate term for lady.) They also look after the management of numerous women engaged in the public kitchen and other departments of the Dera. These women are all spiritually minded, advanced souls and serve with a loving devotion that is rare on this earth. Of course, they get no financial pay. They get only their food from the public kitchen and their rooms. Yet they would not give up their present jobs for the salary of the Governor General, with all its honors and emoluments. They consider that they are serving the King of kings.

8. There are many others who deserve mention. Among them are Raja Ram of Rawalpindi, a manufacturing jeweler and banker, and Shiv Shankar of Amritsar, a rich merchant, who have both built magnificent and expensive halls in their own towns devoted to our Master's work. They are unassum-

ing, humble, and beautiful in spirit, and much devoted to
our Master. They are frequently seen in the Dera. Besides
these, there are many other prominent men, judges, lawyers,
doctors, college professors, bachelors and masters of arts,
without number, all paying deference to our Master with a
sweet humility and loyalty that only a great Master could inspire in such men. None but the greatest of souls could capti-
vate and hold such a wonderful personnel as his worshipful
followers. All of these men, wise in their own lines, esteem it
the greatest privilege to sit at the Master's holy feet and absorb the greater wisdom.

Each life is predetermined

One of the best beloved of your number has asked this disciple to try to give more of the Master's own words in these
letters. Well and good. Last month he accompanied the Master to Amritsar for a two days' satsang in the new hall. Late
one evening after the crowd had been shut out, a few of us sat
at the Master's feet in the upper room of the hall. One of us
asked the Master this question: "Is it true that a certain definite number of breaths, a fixed amount of food, a certain
number of actions of different kinds, are all allotted to each
person and all predetermined before his birth?" The Master
replied, "Yes, everyone is allotted just so many breaths which
he may draw during his lifetime, a certain fixed quantity of
food, and all other things which he may receive and may do
during his life. Thus his whole life is set and arranged on the
basis of his past earnings, of his karma. If then he uses up his
allotment prematurely by overindulgence, he cuts his life short
by just that much."

The Master explained at another time that one reason the
yogis have been able to prolong their lives far beyond the usual
periods was because their time was spent largely in a sort of

trance condition wherein breathing was almost stopped. Question: "Then a man should eat just as little as possible and keep as quiet as possible, if he wishes to live long?" Answer: "Yes, he should eat only the minimum amount required to keep his body in good condition. And he should indulge in nothing that unnecessarily causes rapid breathing, or any other waste of vital forces. He should do nothing needlessly that causes any expenditure of energy or life-force, or in any other way squander his allotment." Question: "But is long life always a good thing?" Answer: "No, a long life is useless unless devoted to Shabd and spent in the service of Sat Purush under the direction of Satguru." It was further brought out by discussion that the Master's meaning was very clear to the effect that the expenditure of one's allotment was to be limited to legitimate uses and not to be squandered by any sort of indulgence, just for the sake of indulgence or just to gratify the senses. Only by observing this rule may one live the full measure of his allotted days. Each one starts in life with a definite amount of capital which he has earned in past lives. He is permitted to do as much as he pleases with that capital. He can "blow it all in," as we say, in a short time, or he may use it properly and extend his life to the limit of years.

Great crowds press upon the Master
At this satsang a large number were initiated. The interest was unusually great. Throngs came to the holy Satguru from early morning until late at night and they would have continued to come all night long if the Master had not gone inside and shut his doors. They sat in great numbers just outside of his rooms, waiting for his coming out, just hoping for another glimpse of him and possibly another gracious "Radha Soami" from him. They pressed the doors and windows in mobs, and guards had to be stationed at the doors to limit

the numbers admitted. Otherwise the Master would have been thronged beyond endurance. They almost try to climb over each other to get to him. Each foot of space is contested to see who will get closest to him. But he meets them all, whether one alone or ten thousand at a time, with a fatherly smile and a greeting of "Radha Soami." His kindly words of wisdom and love inspire them all. This writer has frequently watched the crowds thus thronging the Master, many of them men and women of culture, offering some of the most phenomenal demonstrations of devotion. He has many times tried to analyze it into its psychological elements. Often with tears in their eyes, hands folded in an attitude of worship, and on their faces the radiance of joy and love. There is nothing else like it to be found on earth.

The writer has also watched the dull perfunctory ceremonial worship of idols in some of the temples. The faces of the worshippers wore a fixed and serious expression, usually what you would expect to see at a funeral. Occasionally some poor woman, looking the very picture of despair, would implore her god to have pity. Seldom anywhere was seen even the light of hope, much less of love. The writer is also familiar with the customary forms of worship as carried on in the Christian churches throughout the world: the usual awe and hush; the solemn mien and sonorous voice of the priest or minister, as he orates of things he knows nothing about; the dignified formality of the entire ceremony, the half-dubious expressions on the faces of the crowd in the pews, the set reading of the scripture and the songs of the choir, all are carried out as punctiliously as if it were to be their last act on earth hoping thereby to escape the damnation of hell. In the old-time Baptist and Methodist revivals, the above-described ceremonies generally gave way to manifold demonstrations of emotion and hysteria. The writer has also watched the stern and set faces of men as they turned their attention toward Mecca at sunset, and went through with their formal prayers to Allah and the prophet of Islam.

But nowhere has he ever witnessed such beautiful, spontaneous and joyous worship as that given to the Master, the beloved Satguru. In their faces, thousands of them in one great throng, they show combined love and joy and hope and cheerful realization. Sometimes accentuated by tears of gladness, their eyes sparkle as if lit up by the light of the third heaven. Here is worship with perfect understanding, mingled with love. They know exactly whom and what they are worshipping. It is no theological belief with them. Their living lord is right there before their eyes, and he is not a theory. I am aware that all of this is probably beyond the ken of the average American, brought up as we have been upon an unholy mixture of dogmatic theology and materialism. But to these people the Master is all there is of God and of heaven and of eternal life, combined and embodied in this human form. The most astute and analytical philosophers among them see nothing inconsistent in the idea of God and man being fully expressed in one form right among them. To them it is in fact the normal thing, and they cannot imagine the full expression of divine love on earth in any other manner. When they have seen him, and learned to love him, they know that they can depend upon him for eternal life. They know in their souls that seeing him now, today, they have that boundless life already. It is not a faraway hope, a vague intangible something to be wondered about. It is a present possession. And so why shouldn't they be filled with joy?

It would be idle to call this blind devotion. That would be an unfortunate reflection upon the intelligence and fair-mindedness of the person making such a comment. If you could witness this devotion yourself, you would know that it is the intelligent worship of the soul. The worship of the Master is a living joy, unlike anything else on earth. In the master's presence it is all light. No shadow can remain, and it carries with it its own internal evidence of truth and reality. Borne up upon this reality, the heart takes wings like an eagle. And yet probably nothing but a personal experience would ever have convinced this disciple of that sublime reality. He does not expect everyone else to accept it all at once.

The Master is all in all

Under the date of January 27, 1933, the following entry appears in the diary of this writer:

> "This morning the sun shines again in all of his golden glory. The Master has returned. I have seen him, have looked into his smiling eyes and heard his kindly voice in greeting. Life has returned, and the light of the world has dispelled the night of the soul. For three weeks, the sun shone not by day, and the moon and the stars gave not their light by night. The birds forgot their song, and only the shriek of things in the distant jungle broke the oppressive silence. Men came and went like ships passing each other in the night. Only in bhajan was there life and light; for the Master's radiant form is always there, if the scales but fall from our eyes, that we may see. But this adorable earthly form was 150 miles away.
>
> "If any of my friends should feel that there is some exaggeration in these words, let them come in person to the Master. Let them live with him for eight months, watch his gracious ministry to thousands of eager disciples, behold his tender forgiveness extended to his erring children, receive his holy benediction upon their own feeble efforts, learn to love him as their father, redeemer, savior,

realize all of this, and tell me if there is exaggeration. They will probably say that without him, the world ceases to exist and time itself stands still. This disciple daily grows more and more thankful that he has found the way to the Master's holy feet. But the feelings of a disciple will probably remain an enigma to the average American until he himself becomes a disciple and has the same experiences with the Master."

Personal experiences

Some of your number have written urgent requests to know what progress this disciple has made internally. Obviously, that is something which cannot be discussed without special permission of the Master. But this much may be said: This disciple's experiences with the Master, on the inner path and otherwise, have been extremely satisfactory. They have been of such a nature as to convert all faith into positive knowledge as to the Master's genuineness and leadership, and the truth of his message. The immediate future is very bright with promise of greater things. There is every assurance of success. Do not let your faith in the Master waver for an instant, no matter what the difficulties in the way. Final success is sure to attend your efforts.

Cordially and fraternally yours,

Julian P. Johnson

Eleven

The Dera
April 2, 1933

Beloved Homeland Satsangis,

These letters may be a little irregular in reaching you, but I am doing my best to get them to you as nearly on time as possible. This disciple is one busy boy here. I told the dear Master some days ago, if he would give me thirty-six hours a day in which to work, I would be glad to put in more time in the study of the language and other things of minor importance. And let me say right here in the very beginning of this letter that every satsangi in the world who has been so fortunate as to get Nam from our Master should consider it his primary aim, purpose, and business in life to go inside and take up the journey to higher regions. To that, everything else must be subordinated, even the making of a living. And if you make this your main objective in life, you need have no worries about business or other affairs. Do not forget that your Master is one with the supreme Lord and he will take care of you.

A question often repeated
The writer of these letters has been asked the following question with so much persistency and urgency that it seems necessary to attempt an answer. It appears to belong in this series because the students of the Master are constantly

confronted by this very question. They should be prepared to meet it, and it is our fondest hope to help remove every obstruction from the pathway of approach to the Master's holy feet.

The question is, "If the Christian religion is not of God and true in doctrine, how is it that that religion has developed so many noble, self-sacrificing characters in history and has also produced the highest civilization known on earth, while the several religions of India have done little, if anything, to elevate and liberate her people?"

Since the writer was once an authorized representative of the Christian religion, a graduate in its theology, but now is devoted to a faith originating in India, this question comes to him with special emphasis and force. It is a question that cannot be evaded. Let us then face the issue squarely. If the answer startles us, shocks us a little, let us bear in mind that progress, as well as safety, comes by facing the truth and not by ducking our heads in the sand.

Christian religion not taught by Jesus

In the second and third centuries of the Christian era, the religion as lived and taught by Jesus underwent many changes, going through a gradual process of crystallization into a formal religion and drifting away from the pure spiritual precepts as taught and much emphasized by the gentle Nazarene. When that process of crystallization was completed, the product was something very different from that which was taught and lived by the Master himself. So, in this discussion, when reference is made to the Christian religion, this latter product is meant, and not the religion actually lived by Jesus. Let this fact be kept clearly in mind. It may avoid misunderstanding and prejudice. It will help us to get at the truth of the matter.

When that religion finally emerged from its catacombs—

after the era of persecution was over—and was made the state religion by decree of the emperor Constantine a little over three hundred years from the date of the birth of Jesus, that process of crystallization, externalization and formalization had reached its culmination. Up to that time two powerful forces had been exerting their sinister influences upon the great body of Christian believers. One of them was priestcraft and the other was absolute monarchism. Monarchism first persecuted it and then took it over as its darling child. In the meantime that body itself had been remodeled out of all resemblance to its former self. Those dark and malign forces had for a long time, stealthily but effectively, concentrated in Egypt as their center of operations. From there they invaded Rome. They first converted the Roman republic into an absolute monarchy under the Caesars, and then the Egyptian priesthood slowly wound its tentacles about the new religion and finally absorbed it. When monarchism was finally seated upon the throne of almost-universal empire, it espoused its twin sister, priestcraft; and from that incestuous union, the universal church was born. The three were then merged into one body, and the politico-theological institution became the Catholic Church, with the pope-emperor as its head.

This new power, once thoroughly entrenched in Italy and adjacent territory, set about enlarging its powers by converting the world. It invaded Europe. Arius and others were sent out as missionaries. The scheme was extremely clever. First let the priesthood bring the people under voluntary submission and then the monarch will assume control. It was better than conquest by the sword. The Norsemen, the Anglo-Saxons, the Gauls, and nearly all of the Germanic peoples of Europe gradually came under the sway of the pope. They found the field ready for the harvest, for the people of Europe had long ago drifted away from their ancient moorings. They

had long ago forgotten the spirituality of their illustrious pro-
genitors, and the pure simple faith of earlier times had degen-
erated into a ceremonial formalism, having no virility or appeal to intelligence. They readily accepted the new system.
The pope became virtually the emperor of Europe and the
universal dictator. The principle of universal authority became dominant in Europe, as opposed to individual rights.
The church was everything. The individual was nothing. The
individual existed only for the benefit of the supreme organization, which was now both church and state. To more thoroughly establish its authority, it arrogated to itself divine powers and prerogatives. The pope was the vice-regent of God on
earth, and absolute submission to him was the supreme virtue.
Rebellion against him was the arch-crime. And simultaneously
with the inauguration of this universal power began the Dark
Ages, which hung like the shadows of night over all Europe.

Why the Dark Ages?

The thoughtful student will ask, why the Dark Ages? Why
should darkness supervene at the very moment when the
church had every chance to give light? If it were a divine
agency, the moment was ripe for its supreme demonstration.
It had a chance to open up an era of light such as the world
had never known in this age, if it had been an agent of light
itself. But the era of darkness set in at the very moment light
should have dawned. Why this darkness? Note well the answer to this question, for therein lies the answer to our original query: *Organized religion has never done anything to bring
light into the world, to develop spirituality, or to establish and
promote civilizations.*

Its entire genius and tendency lie exactly in the opposite
direction. As soon as any religion is settled upon a people in
organized form, with its priesthood in authority, it begins its

deadly work of suppression, of subjugating reason to authority, of smothering the intellect, and of denying the right of
individual thought and initiative. All progress ceases, and
ritual and ceremony take the place of spontaneous worship.
Innovation becomes a crime against society. Religion becomes
a dead letter, and the priests grow fat. Such is the history of
all formal religions, not alone the Christian religion. This fact
is so well known to the student of history that examples need
not be cited here.

Organization destroys religion

The primary evil lies in the very nature or fact of the organization itself. There should be no attempt at organizing religion. The death of the thing itself lies in the process of organizing it. It is like encasing the entire body of a healthy man
in a plaster of paris cast. It is like trying to build a cage around
an eagle. It is analogous to trying to organize a science like
chemistry, for example, and then building up about it a set of
fixed dogmas and a priesthood to teach and interpret it. The
science itself would be killed by that very process. Organized
religion exerts the same destructive influence upon true spirituality. Organized religion and priestcraft are essentially one
and the same thing, even in its most liberal Protestant form.
If any think otherwise, they only deceive themselves.

Spiritual religion, a true science

But religion, or spirituality, as taught and practiced by the
Masters, is something vitally different. It is a free and exact
science. It is subject to the same analysis and demonstration
as any other science. It is controlled by laws of nature just as
rigid and universal in their operation. Its methods are as exact, and its results as uniform as in any science known. The
fact that the spiritual work of the Masters is an exact science

is quite difficult for Western students to grasp, accustomed as they are to think of religion as a bundle of vague theories and beliefs; yet the lack of scientific value in those theories and beliefs is the main thing that is now forcing the majority of Western college men and women to discard all religion. Their intelligence is forcing them to give up the old, and they have not yet found anything better. But the spiritual Master's position is exactly like that of any master of science in his laboratory. Only the Master is more than a teacher. There comes a time in the course of each student's demonstration in spiritual science, when steep and rugged mountains must be climbed, even the dizziest heights. Then he needs not only an experienced guide, but the strong right hand of that guide must support him in places where he could never make the grade alone. Then it is that the value and absolute necessity of the living Master is fully realized. Then it is that the great love of the pupil for his Master is born. Though the Master has all knowledge and all power at his command, and the pupil may submit himself wholly to the will of the Master, yet the Master never imposes any authority or restraint upon his pupil.

There is one other point in this spiritual science which is apt to be overlooked. That is the fact that morality itself must be made the actual foundation for the superstructure of scientific spirituality. For this reason all Masters insist that the very first step of the aspirant must be to subdue all passions and regulate his life according to the strictest rules of good behavior. He can make no progress spiritually until this is done. This is one thing that distinguishes the Master and his disciples from all others. They have perfect self-control and their characters are perfect (assuming that they have really advanced on the path). Upon this foundation all of their spirituality and their higher powers are built.

Organized religion deceives itself
There is one thing in organized religion that shows it to be an extremely clever design of the negative power, viz., while it is actually the world's worst enemy to enlightened progress, it firmly believes itself to be the greatest friend and promoter of civilization. Besides, it instantly seeks the destruction of anyone who dares challenge its claim to beneficence. But to those who know, this very fact stamps it as an agent of the destructive forces. Truth, righteousness and goodness never persecute their enemies. They seek only the good of all, at all times and by all means. They win by love and by their own innate values. You cannot imagine a Master fighting or persecuting anyone. He is just as gracious to an opponent as to a disciple. His love is universal, impartial, and his light is like that of the sun; it shines alike upon the just and the unjust. But of course the one who opens his heart to it gets the full benefit by it. Only error, feeling its own weaknesses, fights for its existence. And by that very sign all men, if they were observant, would know that it was error. That is one of the infallible indices of the forces of the negative power, and by that you may always locate them.

The original question answered
We are now ready to answer fully the question we started out with. It is this: The Christian religion has never developed noble, intelligent and self-sacrificing characters, and it has never produced any high civilizations; neither has any other organized religion. As said before, their tendencies all lie in the opposite direction. The assumption that the various religions have done so much for the world is only an egotistical claim of their champions. As a matter of fact, they have all been an unmitigated misfortune, and each in its turn has left civilization in a worse state than it found it. If this

comes as a shock to some, it is nevertheless better to face the truth and boldly seek the remedy. If you give unbiased study to the question, you cannot fail to see the truth of the above statement.

The term *Christian religion* must always be understood in its legitimate historical sense, as an organized institution. It must never be confused with Jesus and his personal life and teachings. From the day that it became an organized power, it has acted as all other organized religious bodies have done, to enslave the minds of men. It has smothered the growth of spirituality, even as weeds choke the fruitful plant in the garden. It has stunted individual growth and develop-ment, and it has done its damndest to prevent all scientific discovery and increase of knowledge.

Many noble Christian characters

Some of my readers will be ready with numerous examples of noble men and women in the Christian faith who have served mankind with unexampled heroism, some of whom were priests and ministers of the church itself. Yes, the fact is cheerfully admitted, and it goes down in history to their credit that they did so usually in spite of their church, or by its reluc-tant and forced consent. Besides, it should always be borne in mind that their spirituality and heroism derived its inspira-tion not from the church, but direct from the divine inner light. It is a most gracious manifestation of divine Providence that among all religions and in all ages, there have been many indi-viduals whose love of God and man cannot be questioned, but the beautiful flowering of their spirituality has generally been in spite of the stultifying influence of the organization to which they belonged. So long as men say and do things to exalt the priesthood and support their doctrines, they re-ceive the plaudits of the church: "Well done, good and faithful servants." But the moment that anything to the contrary is even hinted at, the offender becomes anathema, and, in former times, the thumbscrews, the dungeon and the stake awaited him.

A great modern school

Modern missionary enterprises, the building of schools, and many other philanthropic endeavors in the name of organized religion have usually been inspired by a peculiar mixture of fanatical church propaganda together with individual spirituality and love of humanity. Sometimes the one factor predominates, and sometimes the other. As an example of the latter, we may cite a great modern institution of learning, much loved by this writer. To it he is greatly indebted. It is located in the city of Chicago and is one of a half-dozen of the world's greatest universities—the University of Chicago. Although only about forty years of age, its great light shines to the ends of the earth and it has made for itself a unique position in history. Many thinking minds have been awakened to independent thought within its blessed halls. It was founded, promoted, and its work has been carried on mostly by men connected with a certain religious denomination. This church takes all the credit for the institution, when someone points to its noble achievements. And yet the orthodox body of that very church has never ceased to criticize and condemn it because its faculty are free to think independently and to express their findings. They would utterly destroy it if they could, but happily that power lies not in their hands. The great work of this institution has been carried on by men in whom the very flower of modern civilization has reached its highest expression, in spite of the hamper of the church to which they belonged. Long may it live to spread its light among the nations!

A civilization without churches

The question is often asked: Where would the world be today if it had not been for the church? The answer is: It would probably be much further advanced in everything that makes for general enlightenment and happiness. Do not take this as a personal insult if you happen to be a devotee of the church. You cannot help it. You have been only one of millions who have supported the idea of the beneficence of the church, under the delusion that all civilization was to be credited to the church, when as a matter of fact it has made what headway it has made usually against the opposition of the church. If in the last two hundred years certain Protestant bodies have exerted some influence in favor of civilized policies, that does not affect the truth so well established by history that the influence of the church in the main has been on the other side.

The flame of individual spirituality has ever burned in the souls of noble men and women the world over. These divine flames have often fed and kept alive the organization to which they belonged, but much to the detriment of the individual. If only these individual flames had been left free to shine out into the world's darkness, unobscured by the dark and sinister robes of the priesthood, their holy light would long ago have illuminated the world.

The fatal discrepancy

Let us now call special attention to one fatal discrepancy in the logic of those who propound this question. It has already been touched upon. They assume that the religion with which their heroes were connected should be given full credit for all that those heroes did, whereas in fact their major deeds of heroism and service to humanity were generally done in spite of their religion, and often they died as martyrs at the hands of their religious leaders. Throughout history, noble men and women have arisen here and there, not only among the ranks of the Christian faith, but from all religions: the Muslim, the Buddhist, the Hindu, Zoroastrian and Confucian, besides other smaller bodies. Those great souls, nourishing a genuine spirituality born of a close personal relationship with God, rose to heights of splendid achievement.

From all organizations have come men and women who became the world's benefactors in science, invention, in public charities, and even in religion itself. But they derived their inspiration, not from the organized religion to which they belonged, but from the inner light which knows no race, creed, time or organization. Many of these noble men actually believed that their religion should have all the credit. They forgot the patent fact that their religions have also fostered wars— civil and international—race hatreds, strifes, and contentions without number. They overlooked the terrible tragedy of one nation at the throat of another, both professing the same religion, and each side calling on their God to overthrow the other side. How often that has actually happened in history! How amazingly that phenomenon was thrust into our faces during the last Great War! When the debits and credits of all organized religions have been counted up and a balance sheet printed, it will certainly be found that the debit side is much heavier.

The great saints of all ages, including Jesus himself, have generally suffered martyrdom at the hands of the established religion in which they were born. If not that, then at the hands of some rival religion. Glowing with the fires of inspiration within themselves, they set about their work, only to fall victim to the bigotry and prejudice of the organization. But finally, when the world at large proclaims some of these men as heroes and benefactors in spite of organized religion, then the church faces about and brazenly replies, "Yes, just see what we produced!"

The holy flames lighted

When the world is lulled to sleep and stagnation by formal religions, then the supreme Father lights the holy flames anew in the hearts of his advanced sons, in whatever time or land his divine wisdom sees fit. Thus came the great Renaissance in Europe and the awakening in India at about the same time, under the gracious ministry of Kabir Sahib, Guru Nanak and Tulsi Das, and in Persia through the influence of Maulana Rum and Shams-i-Tabriz. A little later the same influence was at work in England and America through the ministry of the Wesleys, and then came the great light of the sage of Concord followed by the Unitarian and Congregational factors of liberation.

These holy men drew their inspiration from within, and their work was the flowering of the living spirit, rising above the cesspools of human slavery and ignorance, even as the sacred lotus puts forth its blossom above the stagnant waters. Reformation after reformation have come in many ages. Men have to be dragged out of the mire of superstition into which formal religion leads them, and they have to be cleansed and taught anew that the source of all genuine religion or spirituality is within and not without. It still remains a tragic fact that the chief cause of spiritual and moral degeneration and the wane of spirituality among all peoples and in all ages has been organized religion.

Again at the Master's feet

We are now again at the feet of the Master, where we started. We have seen that organized religion is not the friend, but the enemy of mankind. It does not produce high civilizations, but it destroys them. It does not develop noble characters, but it tries to subdue and suppress individual initiative. It does not disseminate knowledge, but it does its best to close all avenues of knowledge, lest that knowledge might upset its dogmas and disrobe its priests.

Of course, organized religions have done nothing to liberate and uplift the people of India. They are, on the contrary, the very cause of the degraded condition of masses of people in India. Here, as elsewhere, religion in the hands of the priesthood has thrown the halter over the heads of the millions, and the priests have continued to ride them as they would other beasts of burden. So long as priesthood endures, mental and moral slavery will endure.

What have the Masters done?

And the Masters? You ask what have they done for the people? The Masters have done much that has never been written in history and cannot be written, but no apology is needed for them. If it were so, this writer is not worthy to undertake such an apology. But he may venture a word or two in explanation, so that the earnest student may better understand the situation, and his path to the Master not be blocked by misunderstanding.

The Masters are now and have always been very few in number, while there are three hundred and fifty million people in India. It is extremely difficult for the Masters in the physical body to reach any considerable number of the people. And if they were reached, they are not capable of listening to the appeal of the Masters. There are people right here in less than a mile of our great Master who have lived here by him for thirty years, have seen him going and coming through their villages during all of these years, and yet they do not know that he is a Master; and if anyone should tell them that he is, they would probably pay not the slightest heed to it. Many of them do not even know what a Master is. It is all beyond their comprehension.

Masters follow the supreme will

The Masters do not find it consistent with the will of the supreme Father to use extraordinary powers to upset the usual routine of life and set in motion novel reforms. The Masters understand that the will of the Supreme is being carried out among the people. So they are content to let the supreme Father manage the world in his own way, and they themselves obey with loving submission whatever the Father directs them to do. The management of the world may not suit us, but evidently suits the one who is doing the managing. So we had best leave it at that. The Masters look upon the drama of human life from a vastly higher point of view than most of us, and so they understand it better. They are not in such a hurry as we are to work revolutionary changes. They accept the principle that the supreme Father is already doing the best that can be done for the people under the circumstances.

The Masters extremely busy

The Masters are extremely busy men, working generally more than twenty hours out of the twenty-four. They do not require as much sleep as most others. Our Master here sleeps only about three hours per day a good part of the time. The rest of the time they are obliged to attend to the requirements of the physical body and to carry on the supreme Father's work. They do all that lies in the power of men or gods to help the people. But spiritually the great majority cannot be reached or helped to any appreciable degree. They must first rise to higher levels of evolution by their own unaided efforts.

The Master does not pick a man up by force and transform him. It is always a matter of voluntary individual effort. It is a fundamental principle that all self-improvement must come from within and must be due to voluntary individual effort and initiative.

Physical improvements

As to the improvement of physical conditions, that also must be left to the people themselves. Improvement cannot be thrust upon them against their own will and without their cooperation. One of the most fundamental principles upon which the Masters have always insisted is that each individual's will must be left free to act independently and upon its own initiative. Only in that way can development take place. It has always been the working principle of the Masters.

One other point may be mentioned here which may not be so easy for the Western student to grasp. *The Masters are not much interested in trying to improve worldly conditions.* They pay but little attention to secular education or to the establishing of material benefits for the masses. At first this statement is rather startling. It may seem to nullify all that a Master is supposed to stand for. We are so accustomed to think that the greater a man is, the more he is interested in every phase of human welfare. We are also accustomed to think of material benefits as matters of primary concern in this life. But the Masters think primarily of spiritual benefits. To that all else is subordinated. It is true that the saints love all mankind with an abiding affection that the world can never understand, and there is nothing in the world that lies in their power to do for humanity which they would for a moment neglect. But, as said before, they look upon the drama of human life from a much higher viewpoint than that of other men, and so they know better than others what makes for the final betterment of all, and to that they give their undivided attention.

Permanent improvement impossible

The Masters know that no permanent improvement can ever be made in the material conditions under which human life is carried on in this world. Conditions improve or worsen with changing ages, but no immediate and rapid changes can be effected. Each age has its prevailing conditions of material existence. Those conditions cannot be modified to any great extent. The more one meddles in affairs of that sort, the more troubles he runs into and the less good he accomplishes. If he changes one thing for the better, something else is worse. The present lot of mankind, in every country and among every people, is exactly what has been ordered by the supreme will. If it were not so, the only logical conclusion would be that the Creator has abandoned the job which he undertook at the time of creation and has turned it over to the people themselves, or to the devil, to do the best they could with a bad situation. But such a thought is quite inconceivable to one who accepts the major premise of a benevolent and omnipotent supreme being. Saints do not wish to interfere with the working out of that supreme will; but when the time arrives that people themselves take up the improvement of their material conditions, it means the supreme will has brought them up to the proper time for such a change.

In the second place, if this material life could be so greatly improved that disease and pain and sorrow and poverty could be eliminated and all men made happy in the enjoyment of long life and prosperity, just in proportion as that was done, men would lose interest in spiritual things, forget God and their eternal home, and settle down to a contented sojourn here for countless ages to come. But that is just what the supreme Father and the Master do not want. They want to take souls out of this region, as fast as they are fit, and take them back to their original home. That is the mission of the Masters, and if pain and sorrow are needed to drive men to their feet, they look upon that pain and sorrow as a godsend, even though the individual may regard it as a great hardship.

Again at the Master's feet

And so we arrive again at the holy feet of the Master. The Masters' work is unique. They organize no church. They establish no authority to cramp the initiative of the individual. They give out light to guide all who can see that light, and they lend their strong hand to support the weak who are willing to lean upon them. No external organization is needed. Such organization only serves to draw the attention downward and outward, while the student should center his attention inward and upward. The Master's kind and potent assistance is all that he needs. Any interference from an external organization detracts from the Path and leads the soul back to darkness.

Affectionately yours at the Master's feet,

Julian P. Johnson

Twelve

Dear Travelers on the Holy Path,

In some respects the month of March has been the most notable of all since this disciple arrived in India. The Master's work constantly expands and increases in momentum. At every monthly satsang, thousands meet the Master here and hundreds are initiated. During March almost twenty-five hundred were initiated. And now the Father's spiritual family is increasing more rapidly than ever before.

The Master goes to Bombay
The first week in March the Master left the Dera for an extended tour to Bombay and many other places. He was only three days in Bombay and initiated forty applicants, they say nearly all of a very high class. The number included Lady Joshi, whose husband was home member, or prime minister, to the government of the Central Provinces at Nagpur. Sir Joshi and his daughter, Mrs. Bhide, were already initiates. Mrs. Dey, wife of the Commissioner of Amraoti Division of the Central Provinces, was also initiated by the Master at Amraoti on the seventh.

The Master at Indore
After stops at numerous small places, the Master went to

150

Indore, the capital of the state of Holkar. This place will be remembered by some of you as the place where lived the raja who married Miss Miller of Seattle. They say he has a palace here which cost over one and a half million dollars. But they seldom live in it now, as the raja lost his job as king and now has nothing to do but try to enjoy life. He has a real castle in France, which they say requires two hundred servants to keep in order. They live there part of the time. So he and the former Miss Miller go where fancy takes them.

At Indore the deputy inspector general of police is the son-in-law of Rai Sahib, private secretary to the Master, and so everything was done to make the Master's coming a royal occasion. More than four thousand people were at the station to meet him. The enthusiasm was great. Immense crowds attended his satsangs, and on the nineteenth and twentieth, 1,850 souls were initiated by the Master. This extra-large number were brought to the Master chiefly through the influence of Pritam Das, the man mentioned in number ten of these letters. He used to be regarded as a Guru and is still much loved and venerated by the people, although he now directs everyone to his lord and Master, our beloved Satguru. Here the interest was profound and everywhere the great Father was greeted by throngs of people eager to see and hear him.

On the return trip, the Master visited Agra where he was most cordially received by Sahab Ji, the head of the Agra satsang, with whom he remained overnight. The Master was especially delighted to have another visit with Seth Sahib, a real saint and nephew of the great Soami Ji. His health is now somewhat improved.

Satsangs not united
This may be a good place to say, in answer to many questions, that there is no organic connection whatsoever between

our Master and his satsang here, and the Agra center. There never has been any connection, except that of a similarity of teaching and a common origin. That satsang came down to the present leader, Anand Sarup, commonly called Sahab Ji, through the Gurus mentioned in the discourses—Rai Bahadur Saligram, P. Braham Shankar Misra, and Sarkar Sahab. Besides this one in Agra, there are five or six other centers of considerable importance. I believe they claim ten all together, each with its own Guru, and standing out independent of all the rest. Of these smaller groups, the main one is in Allahabad. There are, in all India, now close to a quarter of a million Radha Soami adherents. It should be kept in mind that in this science there is no such thing as a church organization, neither is it a lodge or an order. The Master is the beginning and the end of the organization, although the general gathering of any particular group of his disciples is called a satsang.

The Beas group or center

Our own group had its inception through the work of Saint Baba Jaimal Singh, who was a disciple of the founder, Soami Ji, but was never connected with the Agra group. And so this center never had any connection with the Agra Gurus. Baba Jaimal Singh became the Guru of our Master, Maharaj Sawan Singh, whom he initiated up in the foothills of the Himalayas in 1894. Baba Jaimal Singh then laid the foundation of this great work in the Punjab, with this little Dera as his center, and here he passed to the higher regions in 1903, leaving his work to our Master, whom he designated as his successor. Our Master is, therefore, the spiritual grandson of Soami Ji, through Baba Jaimal Singh, and has never had any sort of connection with the other centers or any of their Gurus, except that of brotherly love and good fellowship.

Our Master and this satsang have always adhered strictly

to the teachings and methods of the great founder, Soami Ji. His teachings have been handed down to our Master intact by Baba Jaimal Singh, and so our Satguru continues to teach his disciples in strict accord with the teachings of Soami Ji. These teachings are also in full accord with the teachings of all other saints from time immemorial, and from Kabir Sahib and Guru Nanak down to Maharaj Ji himself.

Entente cordiale between groups

At the present time there exists the utmost entente cordiale between the two great centers of Radha Soami disciples (and between all the other centers so far as this writer knows), and this fact was strongly emphasized by our Master's recent visit to Agra. He was with them also during the big Christmas celebration held by the Agra center.

At Agra they carry on an extensive industrial and manufacturing activity along with their spiritual work. They do this, they say, to supply employment to thousands of satsangis and to develop efficiency in self-support. But our Master devotes his energies solely to spiritual work, with the minimum of attention to material things.

It may be proper to say here that the magnificent monument to Soami Ji, now being built in Agra, is being erected by funds donated by rich relatives of Soami Ji, together with some private subscriptions from other satsangis. But in this our Master and this satsang have taken no part.

The Master at home again

On March 23 the Master returned to the Dera from his long tour. Great crowds gave him an enthusiastic welcome back home. The Dera without him is only a place with sacred memories. His loving greetings bring light and gladness to thousands who await his return. Already many have gathered for the monthly satsang. The next day the place is swarming with visitors. Tents are set up and all buildings of the Dera are literally beehives of activity. Porches and verandas are full of cots and mats on which the people sleep. Thousands are coming and going. The public kitchen is cooking vast kettles of rice and vegetables, and great stacks of *chapattis*. The latter is a sort of pancake made of whole wheat flour and is the staple bread in this country. Twelve thousand people are to be fed at this gathering. No one is charged for meals, but each one who is able to contribute to the fund goes to the secretary, and gives what he can afford to give, much or little. Thus funds are provided in plenty to meet all expenses.

The raja and rani of Landhaura
This satsang will be remembered, especially on account of the presence of the raja and rani (king and queen) of Landhaura. He is the ruler of a small state or kingdom in the north of India. The rani has been a satsangi for nearly three years. Finally, the raja himself decided to come. This disciple went to the afternoon satsang, as usual, and took his seat on the matting and rugs in the open compound before the little platform on which the Master sits. Everybody sits on rugs or matting here. No chairs. The people would not be comfortable on chairs. This disciple has learned to sit cross-legged with the rest of them. This way many more people can occupy the same floor space. It is not so uncomfortable as you would think, after you get used to it. A little open space had been kept for the raja, and presently he came and sat down as unostentatiously as any of the rest. The only thing that indicated any difference was the fact that an attendant placed a silk embroidered cushion for the raja to sit on, and a little extra space was reserved around him so that His Highness might not be crowded. This writer sat by his side and pon-

dered how the high and the low alike all come to sit at the Great Master's feet.

Here all are one. Earthly distinctions are forgotten. To the American, it was hard to realize that a real king sat there, by his side with the rest, listening to the Master's gracious message as eagerly as anyone. The rani sat in a little enclosure just back of the Master and to one side, a group of ladies attending her, but with no pomp or ceremony at all. A glance across the grounds showed an armed military guard pacing back and forth in front of the guest house, the only sign that royalty was quartered there. During his discourse the Master said very definitely that all earthly distinctions counted for nought in the realm of the soul. The rich man and the prince, the ruler and the pauper, were all on the same footing when they faced the great future. All were one before the supreme Father, and before him nothing counted but submission to the supreme will, and the practice of the sound current under the direction of a living Master.

At the end of the satsang, the raja bowed in obeisance at the Master's feet and would have caught hold of them, but the Master stepped back and would not permit it. That is a privilege he accords to a very select few, but kings and the rich are not among that few, unless they are at the same time very devoted disciples who have proved their love for him and the purity of their hearts. For three days the raja attended satsang and listened attentively to the Master's words. He was given several private hearings also, with a chance to ask questions. After that he asked for initiation, and on Monday he was given Nam, making him a real disciple. His greatest difficulty, he said, was to give up wine. However, he gave the Master his promise that he would discontinue its use. On Tuesday the distinguished company left the Dera. They expect to return here for the May satsang. The raja has invited the

Master and the rest of us to his palace next fall when, he says, he will have every man, woman and child in his territory out to see and hear the Master.

A Kashmiri pundit initiated

About 14,000 people attended this satsang and at its conclusion 490 were initiated. Included in this number was a *pundit,* a learned man, from Kashmir. These highly educated men are usually so set in their own ideas and vain of their learning, that they cannot be approached with anything new or different. And no doubt that is what blocks the holy way to many of the world's greatest scholars. The very thing upon which they pride themselves most is their worst enemy, for by it they are blinded to all other avenues of knowledge. But no obstacle seems to stand in the way of approach to our Master. He draws all men, from every walk of life, as the magnet draws the iron filings. Besides, the truth of the Sant Mat message appeals alike to both heart and intellect.

Secret of the Master's powers

Some of the older and more advanced satsangis here tell this disciple that the secret of the Master's power to draw all men to him can be known only after one has gone inside and has followed him to the higher regions. Then it becomes clear to him. Looking at him as a mere man, one can form no conception of his true greatness. But if you go inside and travel with him to and through those upper regions, then and then only do you see him as he is. There, they say, it is no uncommon sight to witness hundreds of thousands of souls, all radiant in their own light, but all following him and bowing at his holy feet in loving adoration. They say that the throngs attending him there run even into millions, in one vast multitude. And the higher up you go with him, all the way up to

Sach Khand, the greater he is seen to be. He is literally and truly King of kings all the way through those regions of light. But returning to earth again, he never says a word of all of that himself and appears among us simply as a kindly, patient father, going about ministering to his children.

Gracious God, only to be able to go with him every day to those fair lands and behold his glory there! Is there anything on earth to be compared with that? And yet there are those right here among us who can do it. Why not you and I? Isn't it something worth working for? What has the poor old world to offer anyone in comparison with this?

Love, the gift of the Master
At satsang one day the Master made the statement that going inside and advancing to higher regions depended more on love than upon anything else. A satsangi asked, "Can that love be developed in every disciple?" The Master's reply was very significant and should be remembered. He said, "No, that love is the gift of the Master." Then the satsangi asked, "Will the disciple always get it?" The Master said, "Why not, if he works for it? Everyone else pays wages earned, and so if anyone works for the Master, he must draw the wages due him." It is also highly important to bear in mind that "working for the Master" means primarily to purify your mind and to sit for *simran, dhyan,* and *bhajan.* That is really the Master's work. You are doing him the greatest service when you prepare yourself for going inside. The Master is so immeasurably above us that in the very nature of the case it is usually impossible to render him any service of a material sort. Only a privileged few can ever do that. But the one great service that all can render is the great work of carrying forward one's own development.

In case you may not all be familiar with these three important technical terms, a few words of explanation may be given

here. *Simran* is the repetition of the five holy names, as directed when you are initiated. *Dhyan* means contemplation of
the Master's form, and that is done simultaneously with
simran, at the eye center. Those who have not seen the Master
may feel that they are doing the simran in his presence. Incidentally, it may be pointed out that holding a photograph of the
Master in mind is not good. Then comes *bhajan,* which means
listening for or to the sound current. These three should have
attention at every sitting. If at first you cannot hear the sound
current, you should listen for it for a short time anyway.

The Master on tour again

On April 2, the Master once more left the Dera on an extended tour to many villages and towns. But he told this disciple that he was getting tired of these long tours and intended
to cut them out and stay here, letting the people come to him
if they wished to see him. But whether he will do this or not
remains to be seen. He is so kind and generous-hearted that
it is difficult for him to refuse their appeals when they beg
him to come to their towns. Of course he will be leaving about
the first or middle of June for the hill stations to escape the
excessive heat of this section.

Inexhaustible fountain of mercy

When the great Father had gone, and night had fallen upon
the Dera, this disciple made the following entry in his diary:

> "The Master has gone. His gracious Radha Soami has
> been said, and we are once more left alone with our medi-
> tations and our holy memories. Often this disciple has
> wondered if the incomprehensible mercy and loving-
> kindness of the Master would not some day slacken as in
> the case of all other men he has ever known. We are so

accustomed to witnessing in the average man an exaggerated devotion for a time, only to see it give way later to more or less indifference. After that, each one goes his own way in pursuit of his own selfish ends. But now for almost a year we have watched the daily outpouring of the Master's love to all of his nearly sixty thousand children as they come and go in a constant stream. Daily this unworthy disciple has shared in that love, and—incomprehensible as it may appear to the average American—the volume of this divine compassion grows greater all of the time instead of less. The holy light of it burns brighter every day, as the multitudes that come to see the Master constantly increase in number. Daily the divine mystery of the Master himself grows upon us. But the intellect utterly fails to grasp the full meaning of it. When we try to reduce it to ordinary language and express it in terms of daily life we fail completely."

The river and the holy secret

And so this afternoon when the Master had gone, this disciple turned and walked toward the jungle and the riverbank, where he sat down to think. His head was literally dizzy with the magnitude of the problem. We know that the Master is able to do any sort of a miracle that he may choose to perform, but he is himself the supreme miracle. We know it is so, and yet we ask how can it be? We know he is the superman toward whom all philosophy points, as the goal of evolution. We know he is the embodiment of the noblest human aspirations. But when you stand face to face with the living Master himself, when you grasp his hand, when his gracious smile and loving words make your own soul glad with an inexpressible delight, all philosophy vanishes from your mind and just the joy of his living presence remains.

We sought the riverbank where in solitude we could think, where we might quiet the surging tumult of thoughts that came unrestrained. So we sat down and asked that calm and emotionless river to tell us of the mystery—this river that comes down so quietly from the snow-covered Himalayas. Glancing northwards we can see those majestic old hills, those age-old sentinels towering in their superb grandeur over the region of Punjab, their pure sunlit summits pointing always to the highest heavens. From their feet flows this slow-rolling river, this ancient river that for ten thousand generations has kept its silent way, to empty at last into the Indus and the Arabian Sea. We begged this ancient river to unlock the holy secret and explain to us the perpetual miracle of the Master himself. And the river replied, ever so gently and without the use of clumsy words:

"As the river flows on forever, regardless of the ways of men, so flows the love of God. Be as constant in your devotion to the Master as the river is in its course, and his love will carry you to that supreme ocean as surely as the river flows to the open sea."

But, a little disappointed, we said, "Venerable stream, I knew all of that already. You talk like a preacher. I asked you to tell me more of the divine mystery of the Master himself."

And then the river replied, *"O little soul, why does the drop try to swallow the ocean? Only when you have become a Master yourself can you comprehend a Master."*

And then, while the night fell over the valley of the Beas as silently as a feather drops from the sky, this lonely disciple took his refuge and returned to the solitude of his own room, but pondering still over the sublime mystery.

Affectionately yours,

Julian P. Johnson

Thirteen

Dear Fellow Students,

One year ago today this disciple first met the Master in the physical body. For one holy year we have lived in close association with the greatest of modern mahatmas. Today there is so much that we would like to say to our American confrères, and the words forsake us. The heart is full, but the art of expression seems to be lost. I wonder if I can write this letter at all. When the Master becomes such a large part of one's life, one realizes more and more how impossible it is to tell one's friends the story. He really longs to just take them by the hand and say, "Come, see him for yourself."

Longing to be with the Master
Today I am reminded how for years and years I wished I might have been with Jesus when he was on earth, to have been his disciple, following him over those Judean hills and down to Galilee and Jerusalem, watching his gracious ministry and, if possible, giving some loving service. Often in years long passed, the thought haunted me day and night. But never did I imagine it would be my good fortune to have that wish gratified in substance. But now I have only to transfer the scene from Palestine to India and change the date, and in this good year of 1933 I am walking daily by the side and sitting at the

holy feet of the great living Master. My impulse is to grasp his sacred feet and thank him that he has permitted me to see this fortunate day. Out of all the hundred and twenty millions of my fellow countrymen, I consider that I am the most fortunate.

Today I feel a sense of pity for the masses who do not appear to realize what a priceless privilege might be theirs. They are letting the golden opportunity slip by them. They do not seem to understand now, any better than they did in the days of Jesus, that a great Master is among them. They are so blinded by the god, or gods, of this world that the great light which now shines among them is quite invisible to them. Truly the light is shining into the darkness and the darkness does not comprehend it. Perhaps two thousand years from now, many who read the history of our Master may look back with longing and wish they had lived in his day, so that they might have seen him and might have become his disciples.

Theological misconceptions

But some of my American friends will say, "Yes, but your Master in India is not Jesus. He is only a mere man, while Jesus was the son of God." Both of these assertions are due to theological misconceptions. Jesus himself never thought that he was anything above and beyond the possibilities of other men. In fact, he taught the exact contrary. Get the New Testament and read his own words, not the words of Paul, the theologian. There is not a word in the New Testament, except perhaps one or two interpolations, in which Jesus makes any claim to an exclusive, divine sonship. Such a thing was never thought of until long after his death.

But let us say he was a son of God in a special sense. Divine sonship is the goal of all spiritual aspirations. It is the very sum and substance of all *yoga*, which means union with

God. If Jesus became a divine son, other men can become divine sons. Why any set of theological speculators should ever limit that sonship to only one man in all human history still remains one of the mysteries. This divine sonship is exactly what makes a man a true Master. All Masters are sons of God in a special sense. They have risen to heights of spiritual unfoldment and have united their human attributes with those of the supreme *one,* and thus they have attained divine sonship. They are then no longer sons simply in the sense of having been created by God, but they are sons by virtue of having united their spiritual essence with that of the supreme Father. Aye, they are even more than that; they are practically identical with the Father, because of this *oneness.* There is no difference between them, except that the Master still resides here in the human form.

This is the ultimate goal of mastership. But it is a goal toward which all men may look, if they make themselves Masters, after the example and pattern of their own Master. It must ever be borne in mind that mastership and divine sonship are not limited to one individual on this planet, but it is an achievement within the reach of an unlimited number, running through all the ages of human history.

A serious theological blunder

It must now be apparent to the student that it is a fatal error to assume that there is, and can be, only one Christ or divine son. By such an assumption a man shuts the door of opportunity in his own face. He dooms himself to continue wandering in the wilderness, when he might sit down at the banquet table in the palace of his Father. Besides, for such an assumption there is no rational need. It is utterly without reason or fact to support it. It accomplishes no good purpose, while doing vast harm. And it is a poor and limited view of the supreme Father. Indeed, poor in resources would he be, if he were so limited that he could send into this world only one great teacher during all the millions of years of its history, and then under such circumstances that comparatively few of earth's inhabitants would ever know anything about him. The most ardent claimant of this doctrine is forced to admit that even if this doctrine were true, the entire scheme has been a dismal failure. In the final wind-up, a mere insignificant fraction of the human race will ever be saved by and through this system or scheme of salvation.

Let us therefore discard such notions and come and worship today at the holy feet of a living Christ. Our Father is abundant in mercy, and his gracious manifestations are not limited to any one country, race or age. Let us come and follow the Master now to divine sonship and mastership ourselves. Only in this way can we honor him and the supreme Father and share in his infinite love to the full measure.

All Masters' teachings the same

The teachings of all Masters are essentially the same, though their methods may differ due to individual inclinations and also to the country and people among whom they manifest. Jesus worked many miracles, especially healing the sick. Our Master here does comparatively few miracles. This is not because he has less power to do them. It is because he does not consider that the best method of carrying out his mission. Faith founded on miracles is not enduring; besides, such a method draws about the Master great crowds of curiosity seekers. It fixes attention upon material benefits, while the work of the Master is to emphasize the supreme importance of the spiritual. It aims at spiritual benefits only. It seeks to break the bonds of this world which have held the souls of men in thrall so long, and it aims to lift them up to spiritual freedom. The

Masters have found by ages of experience that the best way to accomplish these ends is to convert people by righteous living, by gentle persuasion, by holy precept and example, by convincing the reason, by appealing to intelligence, by wisely pointing out the holy path. When men are converted in this way, they are ready to devote their lives to the Master's path and to go with him all the way.

Things insisted upon by Masters

In all the ages the Masters have insisted upon three things as fundamental. First, a clean and holy life, free from all self-indulgence in the pleasures of sense, and given over to good deeds. Second, the absolute necessity of a living Master to guide and to help the disciple over the rough ways and to lead him inward and upward to higher regions. Third, the inner spirit, the creative energy, by whose operation and power the individual transformation takes place. This inner power is called by Jesus and his followers the Logos or Word. In some places in the New Testament it is called the Holy Ghost or Holy Spirit. Some saints have called it *Kalma;* others, *Nad,* and yet others, including our Master, call it *Shabd,* or the sound current. By whatever name, it is the same creative force, for by it all things have been created and by it they are sustained. It is the infinite Father reaching down to the individual man to give illumination and power and finally to lead him to his eternal home, after it has purified and fitted him for that abode. Only a slight difference in terminology, but the cardinal facts remain the same. There can be only one holy way to the highest spiritual achievements, to the ultimate reality.

The Master on tour again

Early in the month of April, the Master left the Dera on another extended tour to various cities and towns and country villages. As usual, everywhere he went, great crowds gathered about him, worshipping him and seeking deeper knowledge of the holy path. Everywhere the interest appears to be growing, and the numbers are increasing who seek initiation. This disciple remained in the Dera for the greater part of the month, but finally joined the Master on the twenty-seventh at a little village in the mountains by the name of Chalet. It lies up in the foothills of the great Himalayas. There is really no town there, but a cluster of houses here and there, scattered over a group of hills, all inhabited by the descendants of mountain tribes who have for many years been connected with the military establishment. They are a people with deep feelings and strong attachments, sturdy and loyal, kind and generous. They gave this disciple, as well as the Master, a most cordial welcome to their homes. Among them the Master has a large following. This disciple, accustomed to unusual manifestations toward the Master, was quite amazed at the demonstrations witnessed in that mountain region. We left the motorbus in a deep canyon and climbed a steep hill, perhaps six or eight hundred feet, to a small area where satsang was to be held. Streamers and decorations of all sorts had been lavishly set up to welcome the Master. The Master had not yet arrived in this section when we arrived. He came at seven the next morning. The good people, all devoted disciples of the Master, made us welcome with the most unstinted generosity and kindness. It happened to be the original home of Paras Ram, personal servant to this disciple. He comes of a good family and all of his people joined to make the American particularly welcome, some of them even offering presents. They said it was the first visit ever made to their homes by any European or American.

Booming of guns welcomes the Master

In the morning, just as the Master's car appeared half a mile away in the canyon, a shot was fired from the lookout station on the hill. As he came closer, another shot was fired. These shots were to announce to all that the Master was approaching, and to sound their first note of welcome. The people rushed to the tops of the hills, overlooking the canyon, all eager to see the Master. Many descended the hill to the place where his car was to stop. The people came in hundreds and thousands. The hillsides were lined with them. Old men came, slowly hobbling over their canes. They must be there for the darshan of their beloved Maharaj Ji. It was a rare treat that they were to enjoy, a treat which some of them would perhaps never have again in this life. A considerable number of us went down into the canyon to meet the Master as he got out of his car. There he gave his loving "Radha Soami" to us; we then followed him up the steep hill, which he climbed like a boy of eighteen, to a cluster of houses where quarters had been arranged for us all.

It was an inspiring sight to witness the devotion here shown by the people to their adored Master. It was no ordinary friendship or esteem; neither was it anything like the ovations given to political leaders or national heroes. It was worship actuated by the deepest affection. They all wanted him to set his holy feet inside of their houses, and he tried to accommodate them all as nearly as possible. Many of them had spent days, even weeks, in preparing special decorations inside of their houses, in anticipation of this notable event. If they had been permitted, they would have showered him with all sorts of presents. But that he will never permit. He accepts no presents of any kind. But he is pleased when they show real love.

He does not like them to bow at his feet and worship the outer human form. But this cannot always be prevented. He accepts their love with evident pleasure and in all humility.

One woman here, the wife of a military officer, could not control her impulse to worship him, and so threw her arms about his legs and bowed down to the ground, holding his feet. He gently removed her and told her that was not the right way to worship the Master. She should go inside and up into the higher regions, and there meet and worship the Master in his radiant form. The human form should not be worshipped, he said. But the people will worship the human form also, for great is their love. How anyone in the human form, even the divinest of men, can inspire such love and devotion as this Master does, has been one of the deep mysteries which this disciple has been trying to fathom ever since he arrived in India. But it still eludes his grasp. It is one of the great miracles daily performed by this Master. We feel that it constitutes one of the visible evidences of his mastership.

Great satsang in the mountains

The crowds continued to gather all day long and to spread over the hills, until two o'clock when the Master held satsang. More than eight thousand people were seated before him. In such a mountain region, necessarily thinly populated, such a crowd is nothing short of marvelous. Where they all came from, one could only wonder. From all the mountains and valleys round about they continued to pour in. Many delegations of prominent men, officers from the military stations, headmen of villages (some of patriarchal appearance), and also smartly dressed young officers, all came to pay their respects to the holy father and to listen to his gracious words.

For four days, the Master held satsang for these people; the crowds diminished not at all, but rather increased. Finally, the last meeting was held under a big banyan tree down in the canyon. This disciple sat near the Master's side, and as the Master spoke he watched the faces of the crowd. They fairly hung upon the Master's words. Deep interest was apparent everywhere. Here and there a tear could be seen dropping from someone's face, and then smiles and laughter would burst forth as the Master related some amusing story to illustrate his point. The Master is an adept at pointed stories, quotations and illustrations to drive home his message. He is highly eloquent in the true sense of that term. It must not be assumed that this mountain audience was a lot of illiterate people. Far from it. Among them were numerous college graduates, hundreds of keen brains and critical minds. Many of them were learned in the literatures and sciences of this world.

As this writer watched and studied the faces of the people, he could at the same time glance up to the snow-covered Himalayas, towering just above us. The sight was thrilling. For ages this has been the region of the mahatmas, the forest temples of those great men who have become more than men, and yet linger here that they may continue to teach all who seek the light. These mountain retreats and deep valleys, for untold generations, have witnessed Master and disciple walking their trails or sitting upon some mountain crag, looking up at those same snow-covered summits. But probably never before since the dawn of creation, never since the first Master ascended those heights, have such crowds waited there upon the words of a mahatma. Never before in the history of mankind have such large numbers flocked to the holy feet of a living Satguru, as this American was privileged to witness today. If only its significance might be duly appreciated, it marked a distinct epoch in the higher development of mankind. Usually, all through the ages, it has been only the few brave and daring souls who sought the higher path. According to the old systems of yoga, the path was extremely difficult and even hazardous. But now, thanks to the most merciful

One, the path has been made easier and all may follow it who will. Infinite love has opened wider the gates and now many more are listening to the call and entering the golden gate of opportunity. One could almost fancy that these deep mountain retreats themselves were filled with gladness at hearing the divine voice of a living mahatma addressing the people by the thousand.

Eight hundred are initiated

Finally the candidates for initiation were assembled, after the last public meeting had been held. After many had been rejected, the Master initiated eight hundred. He personally inspects each and every one. Many are deferred. No one but the Master knows who is to be initiated and who deferred. He only glances at each one as they stand in line. It is a deep mystery to everyone else why this one or that one is deferred. Sometimes there is sad disappointment, both to the applicant and to his people. But the deferred ones are told very kindly to come back some other time and in the meantime to give further study to the teachings and the duties and responsibilities of discipleship. Perhaps some of those deferred will be ready the next time or some years later. But the Master knows instantly who is ready now. Only those who bear the mark are accepted. Only the Master knows what that mark is and he can see it at a glance. Everyone designated by the supreme Lord for the initiation is stamped by some unmistakable sign which the Master can recognize instantly. Only they get the initiation.

The Master returns to the Dera

The finishing of the initiations in this village, together with a short satsang held the next morning in a village on the way down out of the mountains, completed the Master's work of this tour. He was ready to return to the Dera the next day, to which a few of us preceded him, while he stopped overnight with attorney Bhagat Singh in Jullundur City. We reached the Dera on May 2.

This tour of the Master has marked an epoch in the history of the Master's work; in fact, an epoch in the history of Sant Mat in India. In my last letter, I mentioned the fact that the Master had initiated about twenty-five hundred during the month of March. We thought that a large number, and indeed it was. But that number was greatly exceeded in April.

Thousands initiated during April

During this April tour, many villages and towns were visited by the Master. He was greeted everywhere by crowds running into the thousands. This has been the banner month in Punjab and, so far as we know, in all India and for all time, among the services of the saints. During the month of April alone the Master initiated four thousand and nine hundred. It constitutes about ten percent of the total number initiated by our Master since he began his work here about thirty years ago. So the devotion and the enthusiasm continue to increase. Such large numbers applying for initiation would have been utterly impossible in the earlier ages and was not thought of even a hundred years ago. But the spiritual atmosphere of the whole world is rapidly changing, and the effect is being felt by large numbers who are turning their attention to spiritual things. This is why among all nations the feeling is becoming more and more pronounced that an era of spiritual awakening is now dawning. And so it is. Old obsolete forms are passing and people are beginning to seek the truth, and everywhere the souls of men are catching the first gleams of the happy dawn. What the future will bring forth only the Master knows. But the outlook is exceedingly bright.

The Master is much overworked

The hot weather is now upon us, and we shall soon be leaving for the hill stations to escape the excessive heat of this section. The dear Master shows the effect of the prolonged strain—continuous hard work with almost no time for rest, day or night—and now the heat is making it harder for him, although he stands it all much better than anyone else. We are begging him to drop the work and go at once to cooler regions. Just this morning he said so much work was pressing for attention, how could he leave it? They are coming to him from all over the country, in ever larger numbers. We begged him to consider his health and leave the pressing work and the heat. He smiled and made only a partial promise. When we told him that there would be plenty of work to be done here a thousand years from now, he laughed and said: "Yes, no doubt."

The May satsang was attended by something like 12,000 people, in spite of the busy season among the farmers. About 350 souls were initiated at the end of this meeting.

I am glad to announce that the English translation of the *Sar Bachan* is now on the way to the press and we hope it will be ready for distribution before so very long. It will be a valuable addition to our literature.

Also, the Master has given his approval for the publication of this series of letters in book form. It will contain a number of interesting pictures besides that of our Master, and will include a brief summary of the teachings of Sant Mat. We expect to send it wherever the English language is spoken, as a testimonial to the Master. It will be the first effort of this sort in history to let the world know that there is a real Master on earth. It will be translated into many other languages, we hope.

Letter from Baba Jaimal Singh

We will now close this letter with a gem taken from a private letter written by the Saint Jaimal Singh to our Master during the early days of his discipleship. He was Guru to our Master and is still much loved and venerated by him. In value, this letter is just the same as words from our own Master. It has, in fact, a very special value to us, since its instructions were intended for our dear Master during his early struggles as a student. It may be accepted with the utmost reliance upon every word:

"Radha Soami. Radha Soami's grace be upon you. From Jaimal Singh to dear Babu Sawan Singh—Radha Soami. The benign Lord, Radha Soami, Anami, is wonderful. There is no name or form there. It is only the transcendent spiritual current. That current of grace and mercy is about to come to you, and it is coming to you. But there is one veil in between still. *Leave thou thyself.* All of the material that belongs to *surat* (soul), *nirat* (the eye of the soul), and of mind, and of *nij-man* (causal mind), and of *pranas* (subtle energy) and body; all of the three bodies you must consider as states which come to you during the twenty-four hours. Do not desire things of this world, of physical matter, nor sensual pleasures, nor any material thing for any of the three bodies (physical, astral, or causal). And do not worry as to what will happen in the future or what you shall do. Leave all of this thinking and worrying. All of this material you got from the Master at some time in the past, and you should keep it all as you would hold the property of another. You should never consider it as your own.

"Now, inscribe the words of the Master on your mind.

Remember to hold in mind that you are nothing. Everything belongs to the Master. 'I' do not exist. All things, soul, mind, intelligence, all things pertaining to the material of this world are the Master's, and not 'mine'. 'I' am nothing. Turn out this 'I' from your mind.

"*Jiva* is the name of the soul or spirit. Soul got mind and all material things as a gift from the Father in Sach Khand so that it might carry on in this region of Kal (the negative power), and by getting Shabd from the Guru, and, attaining union with its *dhun* or melody, it might come back to Sach Khand. But under the influence of mind and maya, the soul has utterly forgotten this command and lost it. And so they (the mind, etc.) consider everything as their own, and under the spell of maya both the soul and mind are imprisoned—by maya, and by Kal who, by putting the weight of karmas over them, has pressed them down.

"So long as man does not stand aloof from the world, by leaving himself and resigning all to the Satguru, he cannot escape from this imprisonment and pressure. Therefore, utterly leave yourself and stand aloof. Think that body, mind and wealth, all worldly material property, belong to the Master and not to 'me'. 'I' am nothing. With this idea perform all actions. And do just as he bids you do. Then he himself will take you with him when he finds you fit. Have true love for the Master and unshaken faith in him, and in your mind always lie prostrate at his holy feet. Shabd melody has been given to you by the Master. This gift is indestructible, and one day this melody will take you to Sach Khand. Every day give your devotion and love to this Shabd-dhun; and for this cherish a keen longing in your heart.

" … You should gladly resign yourself to the will of the merciful Lord…. All should do their spiritual practice every day without fail. This time you have less work, but be contented with that and do your bhajan. Only Nam, that is Shabd-dhun, is your own. So, do fix your attention on it with love and devotion. With hands and feet and the use of the mind, go on doing your work of the world, but give the devotion of the *nij-man* to the holy feet of the Master.

" … Radha Soami to you from all at the Dera. The grace of the Lord be upon you all. Whatever is the will of the Lord, that is best."

And so this disciple sends his "Radha Soami" to you all. Do not forget the injunction of this letter, to fix your steadfast attention and love upon Shabd-dhun, and the holy benediction of the Master will rest upon you.

Affectionately, your fellow student,

Julian P. Johnson

Fourteen

Dear Fellow Travelers,

This is American Independence Day, but I am thinking more of the independence of the soul, of its emancipation from the five enemies that have so long enslaved it and from the domination of the negative power. I am thinking of *the path of the saints,* that Royal Highway which leads to complete and eternal freedom of the soul. I am thinking especially today of the great deliverer, the noble emancipator, the Master, the true saint, by whose grace the sojourner in the realms of Kal is enabled to break the last fetter that binds him and reach his home in the supreme region. I would like to sketch this path today, if I might, and make it so clear that all men could see it. If only we could make it so plain and definite that it could not be mistaken again, even by the casual reader! This holy path should be so differentiated and marked out that none ever miss it. Its main features should be so clearly set forth that it will be easily distinguished from all other paths of a religio-spiritual nature. This path of the saints is indeed unique and individual. There is no other way like it, or even approximately similar. There is no other way "just as good." For it there can be no substitutes; for there is only one Way that leads to the supreme goal.

This holy path is not a theory. It is not a system of beliefs

176

or dogmas. It is not even a religion, although it embraces all of the values of religion. It is an actual way, a genuine road to be traveled, involving of course certain preparation and training as one goes along. In fact, the word *path* is not altogether appropriate. It is more properly speaking *el Camino Real* or the King's Highway. It belongs to the royal Masters, and it leads the traveler from earth upwards through kingdom after kingdom, from country to country, each one more splendid than the other, in an advancing series until the upper terminus lands the traveler at the very feet of the supreme Lord of all regions. And this is no allegory, no figure of speech, no flight of the imagination. It is a literal, actual highway, over which the saints and their disciples travel, passing through numberless and vast regions, stopping at different stations en route. The passage is really a succession of triumphs, for the disciples of the saints are enabled to master each region as they enter it, to absorb its knowledge and powers and become citizens of it. No Hannibal or Alexander or any Caesar ever made such a triumphal advance. The saint is the great captain leading the soul from victory to victory. It is a long and difficult passage, but the saint has been over it many times and he is master of it all. He is, in fact, lord of all intervening regions through which this Highway leads, and before him numberless multitudes bow down as he passes. It is therefore a long succession of triumphs, even until he reaches the grand terminus.

Many splendid continents and worlds

In each region through which the traveler passes he discovers new continents, new worlds, and meets their inhabitants. He beholds their dwellings and modes of living. He studies them, perhaps visits there for months or years before he advances. Then he passes on to higher planes. The journey may require many years, all depending upon the difficulties he meets within himself, his karma, and the general fitness with which he enters upon the journey. But if he persists, by the grace of his Master he arrives at last at the end of the Highway, at the supreme region, the home of the saints and the abode of the supreme Father. And this is the end of the journey, because there is nothing higher. He has reached the ultimate region.

The journey made during life

This journey is undertaken by Master and pupil while both are living here in the physical body. In fact, if it is not at least begun while they are both here in the body, it cannot be accomplished after death. That is the supreme value of this physical body. It offers everyone the most priceless opportunity to escape from the entanglements and bondage of earth and return to his true home above. But if he lets this opportunity pass until death overtakes him, he must inevitably return to this life before he can even begin his upward journey.

Not confined to this body

But the inquirer may ask, "How can you or a saint really make a journey to a far country while you are still living here in the physical body? You certainly cannot take it with you." This question reveals a misunderstanding which must be cleared up. We are not confined to this physical body, even while we are still living in it. You are imprisoned in this body only because you do not know how to get out of it. The body is no part of ourselves. It is only a covering, a house of clay in which we live for the time being. It is simply an instrument of contact with this physical world. That is all. If then we wish to travel in regions far above this plane, where this clumsy body cannot go, we have only to step out of it and go. We need not break the connection. We can return to it when we like, and resume its use. This, all of the saints and their disciples who have reached the first region above, do at will. They are quite free. How to do this is one of the first lessons taught their disciples by the saints. Naturally, it is the initial step to be taken before they can even begin their upward journey. But once gaining this freedom, the soul is ready to begin its long and difficult but triumphal journey to distant worlds.

The reader is now asked to follow in his mind the journey over the Royal Highway of the saints, stage by stage, as it will be given in some detail. Let him make note of its main features, so that never again will he have the least doubt concerning the path of the saints or fail to understand how it differs from all other paths. The description is necessarily extremely limited and meager. Only the merest hints can be given here, for it would require volumes to describe the Way, even if one were capable of doing it at all.

Preparation for the journey

As in all other cases of travel, naturally some preparation must be made for the journey. This usually means the gathering together of a lot of luggage to be used on the trip or at the other end of the journey. But in preparing to start on this trip over the Royal Highway of the saints, the process is exactly the reverse of the usual program—it consists in getting rid of all luggage. Though we may not fully realize it, it is nevertheless a fact that most of us are going around carrying on our backs piles of useless luggage which weigh us down and hold us in slavery. Our plight is worse than that of the poorest porter. The very first step is to break the ties that bind us and rid ourselves of the useless luggage that holds us down to earth. These consist of the manifold evil ways, the gross sins, unholy desires, the self-indulgences, the passions, the love of the world, its pleasures, its pomp and vanities. All of these things constitute the load of luggage each one is carrying about with him, and by them he is hopelessly and literally weighted down to earth and bound here. Until the soul and the mind break loose from these and stand free from them, we cannot take the first step on the path of the saints.

How to break these bonds constitutes the moral philosophy of the saints. But in this there is nothing unique. The moral philosophy of the saints differs but little, if any, from that of all great world religions. This knowledge is a common possession of mankind. No one has a monopoly of the knowledge of correct living. The saints take but little time to inculcate morality. That is taken for granted. It constitutes but the most elementary step on this path. Perhaps no better system of morality has ever been formulated and given to mankind than that of the Eightfold Path of Prince Gautama Buddha. But here all religions meet on a common ground. In this respect the path of the saints differs but little from all other systems. We simply must disburden ourselves of this world. We cannot take this world and its ways with us to higher regions. That is the sum of the whole matter. Disentangle yourself from the world and stand aloof from it.

Morality alone not sufficient

Before passing from this point, it would appear fitting to call attention to one vital consideration, usually lost sight of by most teachers and systems. It is this: *Morality, even though it be of the most perfect system imaginable, and even though its every precept be most scrupulously observed, is not sufficient to break the chains of slavery which bind every soul to this world and to the wheel of birth and death.*

And this leads us to one point regarding the moral philosophy of the saints that must be especially noted. In this regard alone it may be said to differ from the teaching of all other systems. The saints tell us that it lies not in the power of any man to free himself by his own unaided efforts. He is so entangled and bound here by the chains of the five enemies that he cannot effect his own escape without help.* It is just here that the saint comes to the rescue of his disciple. The Master, and he only, has the power to break those fetters. Without him, the individual may struggle as he will, he may fight courageously to the end of his days, and all he can do is better his condition a little, storing up more favorable karma for the future. But in the end he is still bound, and he must return to earth again and again under the wheel of eighty-four—that is, the endless circle of transmigration. This is a vital truth overlooked by most teachers of moral philosophy. Many students boast that man is master of his own fate, that he must look to himself alone for liberation. It is a vain boast. For he will return here birth after birth, age after age, until he finally places his destiny in the hands of a real Master. We believe that this egotistical assumption of many students is a sort of natural reaction against the useless intervention of the priest. But the position of the true Master in his relation to his disciple is as different from that of the priest as day is different from night. While the priest is not only useless but highly detrimental to the individual, the Master is absolutely essential to spiritual liberation and upward progress.

Preparing to leave the body

Assuming now that the outer preparation has been made, that the student has divested himself of all evil luggage which bound him down and obstructed his upward passage, his next step is to close all of the nine avenues of sense that connect him with the outer world, and then go inside and prepare to

---

* A reference to the five passions, described in letter nine.

leave the body. How to do this in the best and most effective manner, every saint teaches his disciples at the very outset. The method is made so clear that he cannot mistake it, and the student is amply safeguarded against all possible errors. He cannot be misled if he follows instructions.

His first exercise is to concentrate his mind at the *tisra til* or third eye. He must pull in his wandering thoughts, restrain his restless mind, and hold it steadily at one point. The mind is often compared to a monkey hopping around. But it must be brought to a standstill, to absolute rest at the given center. In due time, if the process is complete, the individual spirit current or substance is slowly withdrawn from the body, first from the lower extremities which become feelingless, and then from the rest of the body. The process is identical with that which takes place at the time of death, only this is voluntary, while that of death is involuntary. The whole spiritual being gathers at the given center, or focus, its powers increasing because of the concentration. Eventually he is able to pierce the veil that intervenes—which in reality is "not thicker than the wing of a butterfly"—and then he opens what is called the tenth door and steps out into a new world. The body remains in the position in which he left it, quite senseless, but unharmed by the process. He can return to it at will. He may remain out of it for hours, or even weeks and months. The life processes slow down almost to a standstill, but the body remains in perfect health until the owner is ready to return to it.

In all of this the student is neither asleep nor unconscious—not for a moment. In fact, the reverse takes place. He is superconscious. He knows all that is going on in and around him and vastly more than he ever knew before. He is intensely awake and will remember all of his experiences vividly. He is now in a world he never saw before and the very existence of which most people are unaware. But it is a world which impresses itself upon the traveler as being much more real than this world. It is also much finer and more beautiful and full of light. Here he beholds a great variety of scenery, of landscapes, of rivers and mountains and trees and flowers and buildings. Here he meets with multitudes of souls, gathered from every nation and tribe of earth. He converses with them, for there all languages are understood by all. The light and colors of that world surpass anything he ever saw before. All of these things the student traveler looks upon for the first time, and with a new pair of eyes which he never consciously used before. He is now operating in his astral body and using his astral senses for communication, the same as he used the physical senses before.

Our student is now in the position of a man who has been all of his life confined in a semi-dark prison and has just been given his freedom. He steps out from behind prison walls into a beautiful park or garden in front of the prison, ready to begin his journey home. In fact he is now ready to actually begin to live. His freedom is intoxicating, joyous. And he is just now ready to begin his journey on the path of the saints, for that is the way that leads to his homeland. Up to this moment all he has done is to prepare himself for the journey and to open the door of the prisonhouse which held him in. Up to this point there is but little that is absolutely unique in the process of his preparation. Many others besides the saints have reached this region. By dint of the most strenuous efforts and the practice of certain yoga, many of the ancients and some modern students have reached the astral plane. They have subdued but not overcome the passions, and their excellent concentration has given them great powers of penetration into the lower astral regions. Their understanding and their powers over the forces of nature have increased correspondingly. Many of them, rejoicing at the great beauty and

light of this region, have quite firmly believed that they have
reached the highest heaven and that the lord of this region
was the supreme God. But, in fact, this is only the very lowest
threshold of that vast system of heaven-worlds which lie above
and beyond it. It constitutes the very first stage or resting place
on the path of the saints. In reality, their journey begins here
since this is the lower terminus of the Royal Highway of the
saints. And yet for most of the world religions, this is the end,
for their founders never went beyond this region, and so they
believed it to be the ultimate.

At this point the student traveler enjoys many new experiences, so much so that he is quite bewildered. He is fairly
intoxicated with delight. He is conscious of a marvelous in-
flux of power. His vision is lucid. Space is obliterated. Time
has disappeared; for now all events stand before him clearly
outlined, the past, the present and the future. He now realizes the shadowy nature of the lower world from which he
has just escaped. He beholds its pitiful limitations, its passing
deceptive show, its panorama of births and deaths, under the
wheel of karma, or the law of cause and effect. All of these
things are now clear to his illuminated consciousness, and
yet he has taken but the first step. For the Royal Highway
begins just as you step through the tenth door, out of the
physical body, and into the first astral zone.

Student here meets his Master

It is here on the very threshold of the upper regions that the
student traveler first meets his Master face to face in his *radiant form*. From that moment on, through the remainder of
his life, that radiant form is his constant companion and he
may always ask the radiant Master any questions he may wish
to ask and receive an answer. From that happy day forward,
he needs no other teacher. All information on any subject is

ready at hand. It is this radiant Master who now takes command of the upward journey. He will be his guide all the way. A few of the bravest of men have reached this region by their own unaided efforts, but even they doubtless had the help of some men who had already gone that far. A few may advance a little further, but only the saints and their disciples may travel the Royal Highway to the higher regions. Fortunate indeed is the student who has a real saint as his Master. For he alone will reach his home in the exalted planes of the region of truth.

The Shabd or sound current

It is quite necessary to call attention here to the sound current. For that is a vital factor in the path of the saints. From the very first, the disciple begins to listen for its sound, during his hours of sitting. By and by he will come to hear it at any and all times, even while he is about his daily duties. Gradually the sound becomes more distinct and sweeter in tone. Only when he reaches the first region, the true sound is heard, the real Shabd. This sound current is the most vital factor in his further progress. From it he constantly draws energy, and by it he is enabled to overcome all hindrances and all weaknesses. It is extremely musical, sweet and delightful. Its attraction fairly pulls the soul upward, and throughout the entire journey this sound current is his constant companion and support. Without it he could never make the journey. Consequently, the sound current and the Master are the two vital factors in making the upward journey. Without them both, it cannot be made. These two, then, are the all-important factors in the path of the saints—the sound current and the living Master.

Location of the first region

The location of the first region should be kept in mind. In

the Radha Soami literature, mention is often made of the grand divisions of creation. The highest is that of the supreme being, his residence, and it consists of pure spirit, unmixed with matter of any sort, and is free from all imperfections. It is called the Sat Desh or Sach Khand. In that region, there is not even mind—only pure spirit. That region is so vast in extent that all the rest of creation below it appears no more than a small cloud floating in its sky. It is inhabited by vast multitudes of pure spirits who are not subject to death or change. They are supremely happy.

Then comes the grand division called Brahmand, the middle division. It is of a very high order of creation, mostly spiritual, but is mixed with mind and other very fine sorts of matter. In fact, mind itself is an extremely high order of matter; for it is not self-conscious and is wholly dependent upon spirit for its life and function. This grand division is the realm of universal mind. All souls, in their descent from Sach Khand, here take on their mental apparatus for purposes of contact with the worlds below; and here, on their upward return journey, they discard it.

In this grand division are located all of the heavens of the great world religions, most of them in the lower sections of it. Compared to the physical worlds, this division is also vast in extent and is divided into numberless distinct regions or planes, world above world, and is inhabited by millions and billions of refined beings, many of whom believe that they are in the highest heaven.

Then comes the physical universe, the lowest grand division, called Pind. In it are all of the suns, moons, stars, and planets, all of the unnumbered worlds noted by our astronomers and, far beyond the range of their most powerful telescopes, still other universes without number. Our earth is only one of the small planets belonging to one of the suns of this system. The earth is comparatively but a mere microscopic speck of dust floating in the sky of one small universe.

Now, the astral region, which our traveler has just entered, lies at the top of the lowest grand division, just beyond the topmost border, or frontier, of the physical universe. It lies in a subdivision of Brahmand, called Anda, which is sometimes described as a grand division in itself. Its substance, while very coarse when compared with the finer worlds above it, is extremely fine when compared with the earth substance. It vibrates at a much higher speed than any known earth substance, and its light is much greater in intensity. It has its own laws and characteristics. It is a distinct plane of life and is the first of the numberless sets of three dimensions, extending upward beyond the earth planes. So, even this physical plane of ours is only one of these sets of three dimensions, arranged in an ascending scale. There are other planes of life below us, coarser and poorer, and their inhabitants are of a lower order of being than ourselves. As a rule, the inhabitants of one plane are wholly unconscious of all other planes above them. They live and die somewhat as we do and pass to other regions, as their karma impels them. The duration of individual life increases as you go from lower to higher regions. Always the passing from a lower to a higher plane depends upon the life one has lived and the assistance of his or her Master.

Such is the order of creation—plane upon plane, world above world, universe beyond universe, in endless succession and variety. To break the bonds of one plane and to traverse other and higher regions is an accomplishment. To do so, one has to qualify for a permanent residence in the upper region. He need not stay there permanently, but he must qualify for it. In fact, he must master each region before he passes to the next higher. That being done, he must then learn the secrets of breaking down the barriers in his way. These secrets can be obtained only from the Master. But the way is always open for those who earnestly seek the upward path.

It may not be amiss to just mention in this connection one of the most vital and important principles of all progress. It is this: *Make yourself master wherever you are; then pass to a higher degree.*

Now, our student, having broken the bondage of the physical body, steps out upon the first of the upper worlds. But he has not yet entered the city which constitutes his first real station on the Royal Highway. There are many subdivisions in this, as in all other realms. There is much to be seen of that vast and beautiful region called Sahasradal Kanwal, so named from a gigantic flowerlike light, looking like a thousand-petalled lotus. This region has been briefly sketched by Soami Ji in his *Sar Bachan.* He calls them only hints. They are but little more than that. But let us read what he says.

Soami Ji describes the first region

"I will give you the secret of the Path, a few hints concerning it. First fix your mind and soul upon *tisra til.* Gather together mind and soul, again and again, and bring them inside. Then behold a window, and beyond that an open *maidan,* or field. Concentrate the attention upon that and hold it there. You will see a five-colored flower garden; and inside of that, behold the *joti* (candle or light). Enjoy this scene for some days. Then see the blue-colored sky appearing like a *chakra* (circular disc). Impelled by love and longing, pierce through this. Then gaze at the *joti* with detached mind. Hear the unending bell sound and become absorbed in it. Next you will hear the conch. Let yourself become saturated with it."

This description is quite incomplete, of course. It omits to mention thousands of things of the most absorbing interest. In that region are suns and moons and stars. In fact, many of them are seen before you reach the real Sahasradal Kanwal. There are people of many sorts, living in different styles and engaged in various occupations—of course, not of a commercial nature. Mostly, they spend their time in concentration, meditating upon the lord of that region. For this, as all other regions, has its own lord or ruler, and he is the creator of all below him, including the physical universe. He derives his powers from the lord next above him. It is not surprising that he is often mistaken for the supreme Lord of the entire universe of universes, by those who go no further than his region and who know of nothing beyond that.

Just before the first region, near the entrance to this region at Ashtdal Kanwal, the student first meets the radiant form of the Master. From here on they make the journey together. Let us now proceed to the second stage.

Region number two, Trikuti

With our great captain in command, we resume our journey. He alone knows the Way, and he alone has the key to all regions, for he has traveled them all many times; and besides, he is the recognized lord of them all for the time being. The true saint is King of kings, and is universally recognized as lord because he is one with the Supreme. His power and authority are recognized all along the route. All other lords, rulers and people pay obeisance to him. Under his protection we now enter Trikuti, the second stage on our journey. Here we may rest and study for a long time, even years. There is much here to absorb one's attention; besides, one has to himself grow and develop before he can advance. Let us quote a brief description of this region from Soami Ji:

"Now, my dear companion, prepare to enter the second stage. Behold Trikuti, the abode of the Guru, where the sound of Onkar is heard perpetually resounding. Then you go on up and open a gate and enter Bunk Nal (the Crooked Tunnel), passing on to the other end of it. Then you cross high and low hills. Now the vision appears to be reversed, and one sees as if from the opposite side of the veil which he has penetrated. Looking upward, he passes into a fortlike region which he enters and becomes master of it. He reigns there as lord of that region. Here the soul becomes adorned with the attributes of devotion and faith. Here the seed of all karma is burned, destroyed. You will see thick dark clouds, from which peals of thunder constantly resound. When rising above these dark clouds, behold, the entire sphere is red, with the beautiful red sun in the center imparting its color to everything.

"This is where the Guru really gives Nam, for the Master's *Shabd roop* is here. This Shabd is, in fact, the Fifth Veda. Here you will see the red four-petalled lotus spoken of by the saints, the details and colors becoming visible as one comes nearer to it. Here the bell and conch sounds are left behind and the sound of *mardang* (like a drum) is heard.

"After that, the soul resumes its upward journey. Now comes the sound of a huge drum, beaten incessantly. Here the soul has grasped the primal current, from which all creation emanates. Innumerable suns and moons are seen here and many kinds of skies, filled with stars. The soul here realizes its complete separation from Pind and rises to the upper Brahmand, as if intoxicated with joy. He sees and traverses deserts and mountains and gardens. In the gardens are flowers arranged in artistic designs and groups everywhere. Canals and rivulets of transparent water are flowing in abundance. Then he approaches an ocean, which he crosses by means of a bridge. He then beholds the three mountains, or prominences, called Mer, Sumer, and Kailash. (From these the region is named.) After this, he passes on to a region of the most unalloyed delight."

Again, necessarily much has been omitted. Volumes could be written and still tell but little of the worlds crossed by the saints. Much of it cannot be told in mortal language, because we have nothing like it here with which to compare it. So we must pass on along this Royal Highway of the saints. They have given us only hints, just a word here and there. Having reached this region, the soul finds itself in possession of new powers and understanding never realized before. In fact, the disciple has to grow as he advances. That is one reason it often takes years to reach the higher regions. He must be fitted for their higher and purer atmosphere. Each successive stage brings him just that much nearer to sainthood itself. But very few of the ancient yogis, seers and prophets ever reached this second region. And yet, no doubt, each one thought he had reached the highest, the abode of the Supreme. For so it appeared to him. In his delight, he could not imagine anything greater, and he had no Guru to instruct him concerning the many worlds beyond. Traveling alone, no one can hope to go beyond the upper frontiers of the first region. A few of the *yogishwars* reached the second, and still fewer the third, by the aid of their Gurus who had gone that far ahead of them. Beyond that, none but the saints and their disciples have ever gone. From this second region the Vedas emanated, and consequently they know of nothing beyond it, although Lord Krishna hints at a higher region when he tells his disciple, Arjun, to transcend the Vedas. They believed it to be the ultimate region and its lord they accepted as the supreme being.

Region number three

Let us now enter the third region. The student may perchance abide in the second region for years before he advances to the next. But as we are now traveling in imagination only, we may proceed. Quoting again from Soami Ji, we read as follows:

> "Now the soul goes on up and opens the third veil and hears the voice of the Sunn region. This is Daswan Dwar, with very brilliant light. The regions of Sahasradal Kanwal and Trikuti have been left behind. The soul here bathes in Mansarover (Lake of Nectar) and joins the group of *hansas* (swans). The soul then circles about and rises to the top of Sunn, and there hears the *kingri* and *sarangi* (stringed instruments, something like a guitar).
>
> "After hearing this sound he penetrates and crosses Tribeni (a place where three streams meet), there entering the vestibule of Maha Sunn, where he picks up the secret knowledge. This great sphere alone is seventy *palangs** in circumference and in this sphere there is at first pitch darkness. Four sound currents are heard emanating from invisible sources, the music varying, every minute changing in tone. The sound of the *jhankar* predominates and is indescribable in mortal language. One hears them and is entranced by their sweetness. Here are five egg-shaped regions or worlds all full of a variety of creations, and each is permeated by and governed by a Brahm. How can one describe the beauty of these creations? Each has its own predominating color, like green or yellow or even white. They are quite vast in extent, in comparison with which the entire universe below Trikuti appears very insignificant."

---

* *Palang*, a unit of measurement of such scale there is no comparison.

Students who attain this third region gain corresponding increase of power and understanding in proportion as this region is vast in extent beyond those below it. But there is constantly increasing difficulty as one goes on up in giving expression to anything relating to those higher regions. They are further removed from the earth and its language, even its ideas. The very ideas in those upper regions are beyond the grasp of the earth's inhabitants until those regions have been traversed, and then one is unable to put them into earthly language.

Crossing this third region not only indicates another stage passed on our journey but it marks a distinct epoch in the progress of the soul. Here he leaves the last remnant of earthly impurities, and the last of his three bodies in which he lives and operates while here. In this region, wholly purified, the soul for the first time sees itself as it is, pure spirit, a child of the supreme Lord. So here for the first time it truly knows itself. Here for the first time it is absolutely untrammeled and free. And from here on, its tendencies are all upward instead of downward. The attraction of the still-higher regions becomes overwhelming and the soul is impatient to go on. From here he returns no more to be born in the flesh—except those who come on special missions of redemption. Being now free from all impurities, the soul here attains a brilliance equal to twelve of our suns, and now it rises rapidly to the more-perfect regions above. Let us then resume our journey. We traverse almost measureless space and approach the fourth region.

Region number four
Quoting again from the descriptions of Soami Ji, we read:

"Now prepare for the fourth stage, O soul, and catch the Sound. Cross the pass above the Hansni tunnel and enter the Rukmini tunnel, where you will see a strange and beautiful mark, or structure, seeing which, the *surat* (power to hear) and the *nirat* (power to see) both attain peace and rest satisfied. On the right side there are bright islands, and on the left are many continents covered with palaces, appearing as if made of pearls, having their top stories made of rubies and studded with emeralds and diamonds. This innermost secret I have described. Only the brave spirit may venture this far. I then saw the Bhan-war Gupha mountain, approaching which I heard the Sohang Shabd. The sound emanating from there is like that of a keen flute. Here the soul beholds the white sun above, with immense light. The region is most beautiful and sweet and full of light. The souls there live on the sound current as their food. Playing about on the great meadow are groups of *hansas,* and along with them are many devotees, sojourners in that region on their way to Sach Khand. Here are vast and innumerable planes and worlds, abounding with a variety of creations, and inhabited by numberless devotees, living on the nectar of Nam."

Kabir Sahib also mentions in this region eighty-eight thousand islands or continents, all set with beautiful palaces, as above described. This region is truly the gateway to the mansion of the Lord of Sach Khand. It is the vestibule to the supreme grand division of creation.

The approach to the fourth region is guarded by a zone of such deep, dense darkness that none but a pure saint may ever cross it. Only he has the light and the power to cross it and to take his disciples with him. By his grace, therefore, we have come thus far, and now let us enter the gateway of the supreme Lord of Sach Khand. He is the great Father and the Lord of us all and of all regions below him. He is boundless love and light. It is said by both Kabir Sahib and Soami Ji that his brilliance is so great, so intense, that even one hair on his body (although in reality he has no form) radiates a light equal to that of many millions of suns combined. It is utterly beyond comprehension; but let us now enter his region.

Region number five

Soami Ji, with increasing difficulty of expression, has given a few hints concerning this region. We read:

> "In the fifth region is a fortlike place wherein is situated the throne of the King of kings. You should know him as the true King. The soul now advances to a great and wonderful field, or park, the scenery of which is absolutely indescribable. There is also a great reservoir, from below which flow abundant streams of the most delicious nectar, and this nectar flows out through large canals to supply distant regions. Golden palaces are set in open fields of silvery light. But the landscape is indescribable, and the beauty of the *hansas* living there is incomprehensible, the brilliance of each one being equal to the combined light of sixteen suns and moons.
>
> "The soul then passes on up to the real entrance. The watchers by the gates are the *hansas*. Here the Sahaj Surat asks the soul, 'How have you managed to reach this region?' The newcomer replies, 'I came across a saint and he gave me knowledge of this region.' Saying this, the soul then pushes on and enjoys the *darshan* of Sat Nam, and rejoices with an exceeding great joy. A voice then emanates from within the lotus, saying: 'Who are you, and what purpose or object brings you here?' He answers, 'I met the Satguru and he gave me full instructions. Through his kindness I now have the privilege of your *darshan*.'

From this *darshan* the soul derives immense pleasure. Sat Purush then speaks of the mysteries of Alakh Lok, and with his own powers and love, he aids the soul to make further advance toward the still higher regions."

Our traveler has now reached the highest grand division of creation, the region of immortality and of truth. While still in the lower regions of Brahmand, he is always liable to return to earth, and to rebirth and death—the wheel of eighty-four. But when he reaches this pure region of Sat Lok, the first plane of which is called Sach Khand, there is no more return to earth, except as a redeemer. Here the student traveler enters upon the full reward of his long and arduous course of training. He becomes a saint himself, and the mission of his Guru is finished, so far as this journey is concerned. But the soul has yet to travel over the most sublime and beautiful part of his journey. Above Sach Khand there are three other planes or regions, of utterly inconceivable splendor. But from here on, the great Father of Sach Khand takes over the responsibility of guiding the soul to the end of his journey. By his great love and light, he directs the advancing traveler through all of those exalted regions. First he becomes united in a mystic way with the very essence of the great Sat Purush and, so becoming one with him, partakes of all his attributes. He then advances to the three remaining regions.

The three higher regions
The next one is Alakh Lok, presided over by the Alakh Purush, and the next after that is Agam Lok, presided over by Agam Purush. Finally, the traveler arrives at the end of his journey, the region of the nameless *one,* or of Radha Soami, the supreme Lord of all that exists. Although the name *Radha Soami* may be ascribed to him, it is fully recognized that no name

can describe him. No thought can embrace him. No language can tell of him. He is the formless, all-embracing *one*. He is the impersonal, infinite ocean of love. From him flows all life and spirituality, all truth, all reality. He is all wisdom and love and power. All visible lords of all regions are his manifestations—he taking form, many forms, in order that his gracious purposes might be carried out in all creation. They are all his forms; but none of them expresses his totality. He may take millions of forms but he himself remains formless, impersonal, all-pervading. He is universal spirit, universal life. Why multiply words? No one can tell of him.

When the traveler reaches this supreme region, called by Soami Ji the regionless region, he is so absorbed in its joys, so lost in its unutterable splendor, that he at once realizes the futility of even attempting to tell the story to earthbound people. Say what he may, they can form no conception of that region or the life there. Soami Ji finishes his descriptions by saying:

> "The beauty of Alakh Lok is utterly incomprehensible. The soul, unable to describe those regions, goes on up and sees the Alakh Purush, the Agam Purush, and then the monarch of all, Radha Soami. From one step to another the soul beholds strange things which cannot be described in human language. Every region and everything is utterly beyond words. What beauty and glory! How can I describe them? There is nothing here to convey the idea. I am helpless.

> "The soul has now seen the three regions above Sach Khand, and the ruling Purush in each one. He has seen them and united his own being with them. All he can say is that here in these holy regions, *love plays the supreme part. It is all love.* So says Radha Soami."

We are now at the terminus of the Royal Highway of the saints. We have finished the journey we set out upon, from the common level of earth life. It has been a journey of the greatest glory and triumph. It has led us stage by stage from the low levels of earth to the highest conceivable realm of bliss. The traveler, the student, by virtue of his advancement, has changed from the status of a mere man, crawling in the dust of earth, to a real god of such unclouded glory, wisdom and power that no language can recount his triumphs. What he has now become must forever remain quite inconceivable to the ordinary earth man. He may catch only a few glimmerings of it.

And this is the path of the saints. Among all of the systems of religion or philosophy that have ever engaged the thought of men, is there anything comparable to the achievements of this path?

The position of the Master, or saint, must now be apparent. The journey to the higher regions can never be made without him, either in this life or after death. Therefore the saint is the supreme necessity, if one is to reach those regions. For this reason, the way to those regions is called the path of the saints. The entire science is called Sant Mat, or the teaching of the saints. Happy indeed is the soul who takes shelter with a saint and undertakes the journey in company with him. Among all the sons of men, he is the most fortunate.

With greetings of love and all good will, believe me,
Your grateful fellow student,

Julian P. Johnson

Gist of Sant Mat

THE YOGA OF THE SOUND CURRENT

A brief statement of
the Sant Mat system
of spiritual science

Sant Mat or The Teachings of the Saints
THE NEW PSYCHOLOGY

This little volume is in the nature of a personal testimonial to one of the greatest of Masters. After twenty-six months in daily personal association with him, and of the most critical study it is possible for a scientifically trained man to make of another human being, the writer sends out this testimonial with the utmost confidence that he is bearing witness to the mastership of one of the greatest, if not the very greatest, of all mahatmas who have ever graced this world with their loving presence.

The Master critically studied

While the author's love for the Master has become the dominant factor in his life, it is believed that this love has in no way biased his estimate of the Master. He has shut his eyes to no facts which could be discovered. He has sought for evidence, both for and against. He has weighed in the balance carefully all points. He has watched keenly every little incident of the Master's life. He has carefully studied the Master's reactions under all circumstances, extending from his enthusiastic reception by multitudes of ten to fifteen thousand people, down to a personal attack by a hostile critic.

He has watched the Master while talking, eating, sleeping, walking among crowds and climbing mountains, traveling in motorcars and railway trains, and horseback riding. He has watched people worshipping him with the profoundest adoration, and he has seen others abusing him and seeking arguments with loud and bitter denunciations. He has seen the Master at the bedside of the sick and dying and at the funeral pyre of the dead. He has seen him enter and has followed him into the hovels of the poor, and he has gone with him into the mansions of the rich.

He has witnessed many occasions when large numbers of prominent men, such as lawyers, doctors, judges, college professors, and even rajas and their ranis, have all sat at his feet with rapt attention. He has watched the Master carry on his heavy daily duties in the sweltering heat of summer, and he has stood by him in the chilling winds of winter, noting how calmly he meets all conditions and works on tirelessly.

In all things, under all circumstances, he has never seen the Master at fault, so far as he could tell. He has never seen the Master exhibit any of the ordinary weaknesses of common men. As a man the Master is perfect, so far as twenty-six months of careful observation can determine. And as a Master, the preceding pages tell their own story.

Some astounding facts

One of the most astonishing things connected with this science is the fact that it has no priest, no dogma, no ritual, no ceremony, and nothing to be believed without evidence. Its entire structure is based upon positive knowledge which any student may demonstrate for himself. This is almost beyond the conception of the Western student, accustomed as he is to mere beliefs in matters of religion. But the fact is that this is not a faith or a religion in the ordinary sense of those terms. It is strictly an experimental science, just as much as is chemistry or any of the applied sciences.

Another astounding feature of this system is its psychology. If you will turn to your standard dictionary, you will read that psychology is "the science of the mind or soul and of its functions." The science is thus confused at the very outset by using the terms soul and mind synonymously. The word is taken from the Greek, which means soul—not mind at all. But many modern students and writers on the subject know no distinction between the two. At best they consider the mind but a function of the soul. Some others deny the soul altogether; and a few even question whether there is a mind at all, aside from the physical brain and its functions. Most modern writers make psychology almost purely a science of the mind. They have thus usurped the name and given it a significance which Plato, Aristotle and Socrates never dreamed of. To them all, *psyche* was that beautiful divine spark which never experienced death, even though all else might perish.

Now, it must be evident that any accurate science of psychology must deal with both mind and soul. And this is exactly what the science of the Masters accomplishes. It is, therefore, the only exact psychology. And if we were to give this science an accurately descriptive name, it would be "the psychology of the Masters." In this system, then, ethics would become but a subdivision of the great science of the soul. If only the Western student could grasp this stupendous fact, his psychology would enter upon a new and glorious era.

But one thing which will astonish the Western student, and may possibly at first be difficult for him to concede, is the fact that the mind and the soul are two distinct and separate entities. The mind itself is material—of course, of a very highly refined order. But the mind has no independent self-consciousness. It cannot function alone, being wholly dependent upon spirit to activate it. It is no more a part of the essential being of man than is his body. The mind is only another instrument which the soul utilizes for its contacts with material planes of life. When in the course of its devel-

opment and ascension to higher regions, it transcends the
realms of matter, it discards the mind as of no further use to
it, just as it discards the physical body when it leaves this plane.

Strange as it may sound to the Western student, the individual spirit is freer, happier and wiser when it no longer has
any mind to encumber its activities and limit its perceptions.
This may sound like utter nonsense to the student trained in
the ideas of the West. But it is a fact, nevertheless, which every
student of this science may and does prove for himself as he
advances to higher regions. He does not prove this by any
reasoning process, but by actual demonstration and personal
experience. There comes a time when he literally lays aside
the mind and discards it entirely, leaving it behind as an instrument which he no longer needs and which is more or less
cumbersome, as the body is. From that time on, the spirit or
soul knows all things by direct perception, and the range of
its perception is vastly increased. But that can happen only
when the soul has entered the realm of pure spirit and has
left the regions of matter far behind.

Some of these ideas may be quite unthinkable to the Western mind. They will probably think that I have at least mis-
laid my own mind, if I have not entirely lost it, when I set out
to make this statement. But that is because their minds are
full of the old misconceptions. My only purpose here is to
state that this science offers to the world a new psychology,
which is at the same time the oldest psychology on earth. For
it has been taught by all of the Masters of the East for countless ages.

The problem of evil solved

Another astounding thing about this science of the Masters
is that it offers for the first time in history an adequate solution of the problem of evil. That is to say, in all history this is

the only solution that has ever been offered which satisfies the demands of both reason and fact. Around this problem wordy battles have been fought ever since man began to think. Mountains of books have been written. But the books have been mostly efforts to fit the facts into some preconceived theory, with the inevitable result that the problem was left just where it was before, only perhaps a bit worse confounded.

Many a poor student has wrecked both character and reason on the rock of this gigantic problem. Others have given up in despair, forced to the conclusion that there can be no such thing as a just God in the universe. For the student can never reconcile the existing conditions of life here with the idea of a beneficent, all-wise and all-loving Creator in charge. He may, indeed, shut his eyes to the facts and end up, like the Puritans of old, by rejoicing with his God over the tortures of the damned in hell. Otherwise, he can hardly find a solution that satisfies his conscience.

Some have taken to another alternative, quite as absurd, and have denied the very existence of evil. In a broad and metaphysical sense, the latter concept is quite true. But it must be understood to be true only in the sense that whatever system the supreme Father has instituted must be the best, and in the end makes for the highest good of all. But to deny the existence of what men term evil in this world—involving pain, sorrow and death—is manifestly to shut one's eyes to the facts before him.

Now, here is a science which offers a perfect solution of the problem. The key to its solution lies in the fact that this world, the entire physical universe, was created and is now ruled over, not by the supreme Lord of all creation, but by a subordinate who is himself imperfect. Hence if you are forced to the conclusion that the creator and lord of this world is not and cannot be all love and goodness, you are quite right.

But if you say that this is only pushing the question back a little and does not offer a final solution, we still reply that the system has been established by the all-wise supreme will and is the best possible system for the fulfillment of the supreme will.

This world is a theater of pain and struggle and death, and it is necessarily imperfect from the standpoint of our immediate happiness. So is a jail, a reformatory, or a hospital. The fact is that this world is not, and never was intended to be, a place of unmixed happiness. It was never meant to be so. The lord of the region, himself being imperfect, finds it his primary business to keep souls here as long as he can, and subjugate them until they learn enough to seek a way out. And that was what he was put in charge of this region for. When men reach this stage, they have accomplished their periods of discipline. Their evolution here is finished, and they are ready for advancement to higher regions. The purpose for which they were originally sent into this region of sorrow and pain has been fulfilled, and the supreme Lord of all is prepared to give them a royal welcome back home.

That the great supreme Father is infinitely higher and better than the lord of this physical realm is a concept wholly new to most Western students. And yet the lord of this region is carrying out the beneficent plans and purposes of the supreme Father. This theater of action had to be a very imperfect place from the viewpoint of the present happiness of its inhabitants, in order to carry out the work for which it was instituted; and so it required a ruler over it who was himself imperfect, for his work would not be congenial to a perfect lord. So, the supreme Father made good use of him for the execution of his own gracious ends. In other words, this world is a sort of prison in which we find ourselves temporarily placed. The inmates of the prison being so imperfect, we could not expect a perfect keeper of the prison. And so the keeper of this great prison is not perfect by any means, and yet within the confines of his domains he is the Lord God over all, and most people do not know of any God above him.

If some people, well situated, think this old world is a pretty good place to live in, it may be a wholesome thing for them to know that this world at its best, when compared with even the lowest plane above, is nothing more than a dirty outhouse, so great and multiform are the mansions which the Father has prepared for those who earn the right to enter them.

Now, when men learn wisdom, when their discipline or self-control is complete, they will naturally seek a way out. And that means they will search for a Master. He is the great liberator, and he alone has the key to unlock the prison doors and set us free. Why was the matter placed in his hands? I do not know. But it was the plan of the supreme Father, and it must be the best way. For his infinite wisdom and love would not fail to do the best thing for his children.

In this connection one extremely suggestive fact presents itself to the student. It is this: *Vanity, or egotism, is the chief thing that blocks the return of the soul to God, and the Master offers the only cure for that terrible evil.* If there were no other reasons why individual redemption has been placed in the hands of Masters, that one alone is quite sufficient. When the soul places itself at the Master's feet and surrenders all to him, with a readiness to follow him implicitly, that means the death blow to egotism. From that day forward, love and sweet humility open the doors to the regions of light. If, however, the liberation of the soul and its spiritual exaltation were left wholly in the hands of the individual himself, every step he would take toward his goal he would become more and more vain of his achievement. This growth of vanity would then act as an automatic stop to all further progress, making self-liberation practically impossible. And this is exactly what always happens to those who endeavor to climb the heights by their own unaided efforts, i.e., without a Master.

We may also add that the task of individual liberation from the bondage of earth and from the slavery of the five foes, is utterly beyond the powers of the individual. He cannot accomplish the task alone. No one can do it. The resources at his command are altogether too limited. He must have help. And so the supreme Father has determined that the living Master shall be the helper, the guide, and the liberator that man needs.

Substitutes in religion

It seems important to call attention here to one other thing. In their wholesale abandonment of the church during the last half-century, many cultured and thinking people have turned toward some sort of convenient substitute, such as New Thought, Spiritualism, Christian Science, Theosophy, and Rosicrucianism. Not a few have turned back to the ancient Vedas, and many also have taken to Buddhism. The high and noble precepts of the great Prince have appealed to many. As an ethical system, it is far superior to the ethics of the Bible. Only the Sermon on the Mount, given by Jesus himself, stands out as equal or superior to the Eightfold Path of Buddha.

If we could get the real teachings of Jesus, we might have a very fine system of moral philosophy, and perhaps some hints as to the method of the inner path. But it is practically impossible to secure anything direct from the great Son of Mary. He wrote nothing himself, and his teachings have been obscured by his disciples, and miserably interpolated by others.

But to those students of Buddhism in Europe and America, it is only necessary to point out one thing. They may have an all-sufficient moral philosophy, but the system is lacking a living Master. It is, therefore, like Christianity, practically a dead letter, a lifeless husk. To read it is like picking up beautiful shells by the shores of some ancient sea. They are beautiful to look at but they are lifeless.

Nowhere in the teaching of modern Buddhism, either in the northern or southern school or in any of the many sects subdividing them, do they give you a clue to that power which alone can free you from spiritual bondage. They do not teach you how to go inside and find for yourself that kingdom of heaven spoken of by all the world teachers. Neither do they offer you any help in overcoming the downward sweep of the great currents of evil. They tell you what you ought to do, but they leave it all for you to do alone. And they are careful not to give you the exact method by which the gigantic task is to be accomplished.

They point you to Buddha or to Christ as examples, but nowhere do they tell you exactly how you yourself can become another Buddha or another Christ. They actually tell you, in substance, "Go on trying to be like him. But, of course, you cannot do it." It is much as if you were down in a deep well, its cold waters cramping your muscles, and someone yells to you that you ought to get out of the well. You know that already, without doubt, but he offers you no help or definite information as to how to go about getting out. In such circumstances, what benefit is it if a minister in a Prince Albert coat and white necktie stands at the top of the well and reads to you a beautiful sermon?

All of these beautiful ethical systems tell you what you ought to do, and then they stand by and watch you go on down to hell. They offer you a charming system of moral philosophy—and, in fact, most religions are but little more than that—and when you have committed them to memory

or tacked them upon your wall, you promptly forget them
and go on following the five evil passions down to your grave.

They all lack the dynamic force you need, and that is to
be found only in the Master, the living Master, the one now
in the human body. The one who has finished his work here
and has gone is no longer able to help you. Those who look
to such a Master only draw upon their own imaginations for
help. The living Master alone can render the needed assistance. And that is exactly the supreme value of his science. It
not only definitely points the Way, but it extends the help of
the Master at the critical moment, and he is abundantly able
to liberate all who take shelter at his holy feet.

No soul, no God, in Buddhism

The Buddhist teaching is further weakened by its denial of
the individual soul and of a supreme being. This disciple believes that this is not the teaching of the Buddha himself, but
of his later interpreters. This is the chief doctrine that saps it
of its vitality. They might, with all consistency, add one more
negative to their system, viz., there is nothing else. They need
not stop to ask who is making these negations, for there is no
one to make them. It is a practical certainty that the original
Buddha never intended to convey any such ideas. He was
making the most strenuous efforts to overcome the obtrusive
ego everywhere so obnoxiously present and to teach the oneness of all life.

His followers even to this day have been unable to reconcile the idea of divine oneness with the existence of the individual soul. But it presents no serious difficulty. A single organ or a single cell may exist in the human body, and yet that
is not inconsistent with the oneness of the entire body. Millions of fish exist in the sea, and cannot live outside of it, and
yet that does not offer any difficulty as to the inseparable one-

ness of the ocean and the individual fish. In him we live and move and have our being.

Besides, if they had known the sound current, they would have had the perfect key to this oneness—to the existence of all souls as parts of the supreme one. Here is the divine Trinity—the supreme one, the individual soul, and the sound current connecting the two and unifying them. They are one substance, and the souls have no existence apart from the supreme one, and yet they have their own individuality. Each is merged into the divine whole, and yet each one remains a self-conscious unit of that divine whole.

How much better this is than that cold and cheerless theorem which says there is no soul, nothing but a bundle of accumulated tendencies called *skandhas*. How this could ever have imagined itself to be a soul is not explained. How it could ever get the idea of a soul, if no soul existed, and no one existed to do the thinking, is a mystery which its advocates have never clarified. It is an idea like the chill blasts of winter. It takes life but gives none.

Cannot sin

Another fact most astonishing to the student is to be noted here, and then we shall proceed with a brief statement of the cardinal teachings of the Masters. That fact is this: When a student has reached a certain degree of advancement on this path, *he simply cannot commit a sin*. Not that the power to commit sin is taken from him, for he has vastly more power and freedom of choice than he ever had before. But he can now see the destructive nature and disastrous results of sin so clearly and in all of its ramifications that, for him, the act of sin would be equivalent to deliberate suicide. It is utterly unthinkable to him. If this is not a very practical result, then it would be difficult to imagine one that is practical. That alone would appear to be worth all the strenuous effort required on this path. There is no more sublime achievement on these lower planes. And with it the happiness of the student is so extraordinarily increased that the man of the world can form no conception of the vast treasure that is his.

All the world is looking for happiness, but they are seeking it by the wrong method. They have never found it that way and they never will. Happiness cannot be found in material enjoyments, not in the gratification of the senses, nor even in the satisfaction of the mind. The pleasures of sense are but for a moment and are usually disappointing and fleeting. We no more than get settled in some situation from which we expect happiness, when it changes in substance, or vanishes entirely, leaving us but a dream, a shadow. The whole world is a passing show, and its allurements only lead us on toward some vanishing mirage. At the end of the trail, we leave our bones to bleach on the desert sands. In exchange for its momentary pleasures the world forges around us fresh chains of slavery, and then we go on, dragging our chains with us. But the spiritual science of the Masters offers freedom, everlasting freedom, and joy beyond compare.

How old forms persist

It has always been a mystery how and why men hold on so tenaciously to old religious forms and concepts. It makes no difference if they contain not the least shred of common sense or fact. Yet once accepted, it seems almost impossible to turn them loose. But in offering to the reader a statement of Sant Mat, let me urge that for the time being at least he should try to divest himself of all prejudice and assume an attitude of open-minded inquiry. Shut not the door of truth in your own face by assuming in advance that you cannot learn anything new. To most of us there are yet "many things in heaven and on earth not dreamed of in our philosophy." Neither should we be over-concerned to find that which supports our own theories or creeds. We should look always for the truth, re-gardless of any man's theory.

When you have given this statement due consideration, then if you do not like it, no matter. Let it go. You have at least been fair to both yourself and the writer. If the time comes when students of religious subjects find that they have dis-covered something which carries them a step further toward the great light, then they may relax their hold on the old and take up the new. But this they should do, not as if they were casting aside something false and worthless, but they should lay it aside reverently, as something which has well served its purpose, even as the growing child lays aside his primer when he advances to higher grades. For this also is in line with evo-lution. The comprehension of spiritual truth must always be progressive, the light increasing as individuals rise to higher levels of spiritual consciousness.

The name "Radha Soami"

It has been said that this system has no name. And in fact it has none. But it was inevitable that some sort of cognomen or designation or label should become attached to it. Many insist on calling it a faith. And so the name "Radha Soami faith" became attached to it. But the term *faith* is somewhat misleading, since this system does not fall in the category of faiths, or religions, as they are commonly understood. And the name "Radha Soami" was not given to it by its founder; it was given by Rai Saligram, one of the chief disciples of Soami Ji. But it finally had the approval of the Great Master.

This name later came to be applied to the founder, and then to the system itself. The name has been applied to the supreme Lord; but this name is *varnatmak* (that which can be spoken or written) while the true Name, Nam or Shabd, is *dhunatmak* (cannot be spoken or written). The true sovereign of all remains forever nameless, Anami, for he is above and beyond all names or descriptions in words of mortal tongue.

It was never intended to found a new sect or cult. And this system was not first taught by Soami Ji, as some believe. He gave it clearer and simpler expression than anyone else had ever done, and he made the exercises plain and easy to follow. For this reason only, he is regarded as the founder of the system. He began publicly to expound the system in Agra, India, in 1861. But the teaching itself is the oldest science on earth, antedating the Vedas by untold ages, or any other teaching known to history.

It should be said that while saints of all ages have taught and practiced this system, it was not without reason that they did not give it out in plain words to the whole world. Each one had to be governed by the circumstances and the times in which he lived. It has been only in very recent years that the heavy hand of fanatical persecution has been lifted so that the saints became free to teach openly. Civilization has at last wrested from the priesthood that power which for so many ages blocked the progress of enlightenment.

Sant Mat millions of years old

The teaching of the saints has been one and the same system since the first saint ever set foot upon this planet. It has never changed and it can never change, because it has been a perfect science from the beginning, instituted and practiced by perfected men, who never make mistakes. It is a science based upon natural law and personal experience. The Creator himself is its author and founder.

But in quite recent years the saints known to history, such

as Kabir Sahib, Tulsi Das, Shams-i-Tabriz, Maulana Rum, and Guru Nanak together with his successors, have been the chief exponents of the system. Then came Tulsi Sahib, and finally Shiv Dayal Singh Ji, later known as Radha Soami or Soami Ji, who simplified the science and presented it to the world in practical form, for the larger numbers who were approaching readiness for it. For this reason he is generally regarded as founder and first exponent.

This system calls for no credulity. While it sets forth some very startling statements, it asks no blind acceptance, but proposes a method by which the student may prove every word of it for himself. It offers the student nothing to be believed without evidence, and it asks no favors of any man. It never begs for money for its support; and even the Master himself, giving his whole time to the work, never accepts any material benefits from his disciples.

Sant Mat is not another cultural religion or philosophy. We may truly say that it is not primarily concerned with any system of right living on this earth. The field of its action lies in another direction. If a man is going to build a splendid dwelling for himself, he will not think only of the foundation and, when he has finished that foundation, stop right there and go on talking the rest of his life about that beautiful foundation. But that is precisely what all religions do. They lay a beautiful foundation of moral precept and culture, but they stop right there. They do not build upon the foundation which they have laid. Therein is their fatal weakness.

Sant Mat, however, builds upon its foundation. It builds a superstructure reaching to the utmost skies. And its culture is that which is gained by the ascent of the soul to higher regions. That is the highest and noblest culture possible to man. It is a culture quite unknown to the man of the world, and it is almost impossible to put into writing anything that would convey a correct estimate of it. It is a priceless treasure quite beyond the grasp of those who have not had the experience.

But with all modern presentations of ethics and cultural standards the saints are not directly concerned. Ethics is assumed by Sant Mat. It is the foundation upon which it builds its superstructure, but that foundation is already in the possession of mankind. There is no need that any saint should spend time restating it. He has more important work before him. All men know how to live correctly. If each one would act according to his own highest ideals, sin and crime would disappear, and righteousness would prevail the world over. The world is not in need of cultural ideals. It has them in great plenty.

Let the reader here make special note of the fact that this writer does not mean to convey the idea that the Masters are not interested in ethics or moral culture. The reverse is true. They always teach and emphasize its vital importance. They are interested in ethics just as truly as any builder is interested in the foundation of his house. And their first lesson given to disciples is to impress upon them that they cannot make even a start on the path until the moral foundation has been laid.

But unlike other systems, they do not stop there. Having laid this foundation, they proceed to build upon it. Consequently, while ethics is vital in their system, at the same time it is not the chief interest of the Masters, and they spend only the minimum amount of time on it necessary to impress its importance upon the student. The superstructure or spiritual character and achievement is their chief concern.

It is quite true that no one can take the first step on the path of the saints unless and until he has established his life upon a broad and sound ethical foundation. He is simply told that this is his first step. It is the one primary prerequisite. But he knows already how to do it. He is quite familiar with its principles. All of this being taken for granted, the saint has now to point out the path of attainment. That is his mission.

He is not so much concerned with fitting men to live upon this earth, or the establishment of a moral order here, as he is in liberating men utterly and forever from the confines of this earth life.

That is the supreme mission of the saints, and to that they give all attention.

Essential teachings of Sant Mat

I have mentioned a number of things which this system is not. Let us now endeavor to see what it really is. The great saint at Beas has defined it in these words: *"Sant Mat is the science of connecting the individual soul with its Creator."* This definition is extremely expressive and very accurate. It assumes that the ordinary individual is disconnected from his Creator. Its primary concern then is to reestablish that divine *yoga* or oneness, which in a real sense is the aim of all religions, although they have not the slightest idea how to go about it.

A reunion with God is the fundamental aim of all spiritual aspiration. It is the one purpose behind all religious teaching and ceremony. But the pity is that they have all lost the method by which that reunion is to be accomplished. It has been lost and covered up in the maze of creeds and ceremonies and external forms. And although the world is piled high with books and swarming with priests, all purporting to teach the Way, yet they actually do not know the first step on the path. Those who follow them only become worse and worse entangled in the maze, and there is no escape until they look to a real Master.

Souls disconnected from the Creator

It is assumed, then, that the individual is disconnected from his Creator. Each one comes into this world so disconnected. He runs on for a time, only by the momentum with which he came, and then he slows down and dies miserably from lack of power. During the ages that he has been wandering about the regions of mind and coarser matter, he has become separated from the great central dynamo. He is now like a motorcar from which the battery has been disconnected. There is no longer any spark to ignite the fuel and produce the needed power to run on independently. It is just here that Sant Mat lays down the science by means of which the battery is reconnected and power made available for independent achievement.

You may see at a glance that this is not, and cannot be, a system of beliefs. It is no mere theory. It is not a matter of opinions. It is not a cultural philosophy. Culture, beliefs, opinions could never connect the disconnected battery. It requires a very definite act from the hand of an expert—a concrete, definite act. Only when the hand of the master mechanic comes and lays hold of the apparatus and actually makes the connection, then and then only will the motor come to life. And the master mechanic works by strictly scientific principles and from exact knowledge. His is a science in the strict and technical meaning of the term. It is so because it is based upon natural law, and its rules and principles of operation are universal.

In all ages of the world, among all races and in all countries, all who follow its formula get exactly the same results. That makes it an exact science. Therefore, the results may always be predicted in advance. The student on this path may always know exactly what he will be able to accomplish. He may not know just how long it will take him, for many individual factors enter here, as in all other lines of endeavor. But if he follows the formula faithfully, he may rest assured of the final results, with no shadow of variation and no possibility of failure.

Three great truths of Sant Mat

There are three great fundamental truths lying at the base of this system, and to each of these I wish to direct attention for a moment.

First, the helpless condition of the individual soul. I mean by this the utter inability of the individual ever to extricate himself from the prison walls and multiform chains that bind and hold him in this world of mind and matter, and in which he is doomed to be born and reborn for untold ages. He has wandered far from the regions of light, his original home. It would appear that he has been sent down here to learn self-control; in fact, that he might really finish the work of creating himself through individual struggle.

He is encompassed by adverse conditions, requiring painful, prolonged and exhausting effort. These conditions are needed to supply the urge force to struggle. If conditions were pleasant, he would just sit down and take things easy for a hundred thousand years. But after he has fought the battle to the limit, when he has done his best to rise above the region of pain and struggle, he stands alone upon a lofty eminence and surveys the field of his struggles. He looks for a way to escape, but there is none. Let him struggle as he may; he must return again and again to the theater of struggle. But if he is brave and continues to fight, on each successive return to the plane of struggle he brings with him an earned increment of favorable karma, giving him a better placement.

At last he looks about him and is seized with an inexpressible yearning to return to his original home. He is tired of this endless warfare. The million entanglements of this world of senses are galling to him. He prays earnestly for his freedom. He finds that he has struggled so long and so hard, but has never been able to extricate himself from the Wheel. He recalls that he has tried every scheme, but all to no avail. He now knows intuitively that he never can release himself. So, when his ego has been conquered, when humility is born of bitter experiences, he is ready for the second great truth of this science. It is this: *the living Master is the divinely appointed agent of individual salvation.*

The Master, the great liberator

As said before, the individual has been disconnected from the great central force, which alone can enable him to regain his lost position and return to his original home. He is quite unable to effect his own release. But now comes the Master into his life. The Master always comes when the soul is ready for him. When all else has failed him, and his ego has subsided sufficiently to permit him to accept the Master, the moment is ripe for the great liberator to enter his life. The Master then connects the individual soul with his Creator. That is his first step. He is the master mechanic whose skilled hands are able to connect the battery and give life to the motor once more. In this particular instance, the machinery is far too complicated and delicate for the ordinary traveler to know what he is doing with it.

When the connection is made, he has power to travel independently. He then has the power to overcome the downward pull of earth, and to begin his ascent toward the regions of light, where lies his eternal home. But without the aid of the Master, he could never make that journey. He could never even begin it. This then, is the second great truth emphasized by all the saints—the fact that there is no ultimate release for anyone from the wheel of birth and death, from the regions of pain and struggle, until the Master comes to his aid.

The Shabd or sound current

The third great truth of Sant Mat is the gigantic and vital fact of the sound current. This science is sometimes called the practice of the sound current. It is also called the yoga of the sound current, or Anand Yoga. The sound current is the most stupendous and vital fact in all the realms of nature, yet it has been almost entirely lost sight of by the majority of modern students.

For more than fifty years this student diligently searched through everything printed in books, to the limit of his ability. He ransacked the libraries of the world, in different languages, eagerly looking for gleams of truth. But never once did he run across a single intelligible word concerning the sound current, until less than four years ago.

Yet the teaching of the sound current has been in the world since the earliest man began to turn his eyes heavenward, since the great Father started the human race on its career upon this planet. Time and again, age after age, saints have come to give fresh emphasis to this great truth; this is the most important of all truths. But soon after their departure, the negative powers begin to cover it up, and to obscure it, introducing a thousand schemes to draw attention away from it. Why? Because it is the one and only way or avenue of escape from the regions of the negative power. It is the one and only power by means of which man is enabled to break every fetter that binds him, and remove every evil that obscures his moral sense or clouds his spiritual vision. It is the one source of help that meets every need of the soul, and it is the open chariot in which he may ride back to his eternal home at the feet of the supreme Father.

What, then, is the sound current? It may not be so easy to define it. It is called sound current because it can be heard. It may be assumed that every force in the universe, moving from a static condition to dynamic expression, is in a state of vibration and therefore produces sound. Sound is not limited to atmospheric vibrations, although our physical ear is so limited. When music is transmitted by a radio across the continent in the fraction of a second, it is just as truly a sound current, or sound wave (if you prefer that expression), while it is in transit as it is when again converted into atmospheric vibrations by the receiving instrument. Only it cannot be heard by the physical ear.

But a finer ear, so constructed as to respond to those higher vibrations, might easily pick up those electromagnetic waves without any other instrument. And that is exactly what happens when the finer ear of the astral body, and also of the still finer body or bodies with which man is already endowed, actually picks up the finer vibrations of the sound current. It only requires the proper training of the Master to enable the student to accomplish this marvelous achievement.

Sound current mentioned by Jesus

It may be of interest to the student brought up in the Christian faith to know that Jesus himself, at least in one place in the New Testament, very definitely mentions the fact that this sound current is to be heard. In the Gospel of John, first chapter, it is called the Logos or Word through which all creation came into existence. It was not only with God from the beginning, but it was God himself. Then in the third verse of chapter three, Jesus himself speaks of contacting the sound current and compares it to a new or second birth. (Bear in mind that birth means bringing to light.) He says that which is born of the flesh is flesh; but it is the spirit of man which is born of the spirit—that is, brought to light by the spirit. Then in the eighth verse, he clearly mentions actually hearing the sound of this same spirit current which gives the new birth. He says, "The wind bloweth where it listeth and thou hearest the sound thereof, but canst not tell whence it cometh and whither it goeth; so is every one who is born of the spirit."

Thus the matter is made very clear and definite that just as the body of man is born of woman, body from body, so the spirit of man is born (brought to light) out of the dark womb of matter and its foul corruptions, through the action of the divine spirit, in the form of the sound current. When that takes place, he actually hears the sound of it just as distinctly as he may hear the rustle of the wind in the tall pines of the forest. But no one can tell whence that inner sound comes, any more than he can tell whence the wind is blowing. Shams-i-Tabriz, a great Persian saint, speaking of the sound current, says very beautifully:

To me came the Sound incomparable,
        which comes neither from within
        nor from without;
Neither does it come from the left
        nor from the right,
Nor from the back
        nor from the front.

You will ask, then,
        whence does it come?
It comes from the direction
        you are seeking to go.
You will ask, then,
        which way shall I face?

The side from which
    the bridegroom cometh.
That direction from which
    the parched fish comes to life
    with the waters of immortality;
That direction whence the hand of Moses
    became bright like the shining moon.
The direction whence ripeness
    comes to fruit;
The direction from which stones
    become diamonds.
Be silent and listen
    to the five sounds from heaven,
The heaven which is beyond
    all senses and directions.

Every moment of life this wondrous Sound
    reaches down from the courts of heaven.
Fortunate above all the children of men
    is he who hears its enchanting melodies.

Jesus, speaking in the same poetical spirit of this sound current, says it is heard in the direction whence the wind blows. And he also says: "Verily, verily, I say unto thee, except a man be born again, he cannot see the kingdom of heaven." He must be brought to light, and that light is inside of man himself. And for this very definite reason he says that the kingdom of heaven is within you. The kingdom of heaven being inside, of course it can be seen only by going inside. And yet all the world is busy seeking it everywhere else. To make the momentous discovery of the great kingdom of light, man must go inside, and he cannot go inside except by the aid of the sound current. Hence its vital importance. In every age of the world, time and time again, the saints have emphasized that one must be born anew—in the words of Jesus, "Marvel not that I say unto you, ye must be born again."

When the soul is connected with the sound current at the time of the disciple's initiation by the Master, that is the supreme moment of his new birth. But the completion of that birth is a slow process, a gradual coming into the light. The Master often refers to the birth of the soul into this world of matter as a death, rather than a birth, for it is in fact a going down into darkness. But the real birth takes place when he is connected with the sound current and, by its regenerating action, is brought into light.

Sound and power through the divine Shabd

This divine Shabd (which means word or sound) may be called the current of the supreme being himself, vibrating through all space, and extending down to each individual soul. Now it has been proved that not only sound can be transmitted by radio but also power can be so transmitted. In like manner, the power of the supreme current can be transmitted to the individual soul who is attuned to receive it. And here is the crux of the whole matter. One must be attuned to receive it. This is the primal connection between the Creator and the created. But the entire process of training to receive both the sound and the power constitutes the course of instructions and exercises given by each Master to his initiates.

In this manner the Creator himself sends out streams of life to the untold millions of beings who are dependent upon him. These streams reach to the outer bounds of all creation. It is the supreme current of spiritual life, the very essence of life, flowing out from the Creator to every soul in the universe. It is the way he will ultimately bring them back to himself, when their periods of separation are over. This current, then, vibrates through all space and into each soul. Anywhere a receiving set is put into operation, it will pick up the currents or waves which may be said to fill all space.

In like manner, any soul when properly prepared may pick up this divine sound current and receive its power. But men have shut themselves off from vital connection with it. It is a living vibrant force and can be heard, and its power can be felt. But first each one must be connected with that current by the master mechanic, the saint. It is largely a process of tuning in, as we say in radio. But only the Master knows how to do that tuning in. And no man can tune himself in. In consequence of man's degrading relations with these lower regions, he has become so disconnected—out of tune—that he can no longer hear the vibrations of that current or avail himself of its power, until the Master reconnects him.

This the Master does at the time of initiation, and from that time on the disciple has only to train himself in that system of scientific yoga, as prescribed by the Master, and sooner or later he is enabled to distinctly hear the sound current within himself. It is at first feeble and makes but little impression upon the student. But gradually, as his concentration becomes more perfect, the sound grows more distinct and sweeter in tone, until at length it is the most delightful musical note ever heard by mortal man. It enchants and transforms him, and by its power he easily overcomes all temptations. It gives him new strength and resolution. It literally draws him upward, and at the same time it cleanses him of all earthly impurities. It fairly recreates him. Under its benign influence, he begins his inward and upward journey toward the highest spiritual regions.

There are five principal regions through which he passes on this journey. These regions are gained by inward concentration, first enabling the spirit to leave the physical body and then to travel abroad in those exalted and shining worlds. These he traverses one after the other, until the highest is reached, the Master being all the while his gracious companion and guide. The last of these regions is in the highest grand division of creation, the realm of pure spirit, the home of the supreme Father. In those far realms of glory, so immeasurably beyond the power of human words to describe, dwells the supreme Father of all. Himself formless and boundless, an infinite ocean of love, yet he takes forms, many forms, visible to his children, fitting himself to their needs, in order that he may carry out his purposes of an all-embracing love. This is the ultimate home of the soul.

Thus the Master and the sound current are the two vital factors in the process of spiritual redemption, in fact, in all real achievement. Without them both, the individual soul is utterly helpless and is doomed to wander forever up and down the desolate planes of shadow and pain, of struggle and death. The soul who has not a Master is indeed poor, though he may possess all the gold of the world. Even though he may be the emperor upon whose broad domains the sun never goes down, yet he is poorer than the lowest laborer who has a Master.

These points are so vital and all-important, I am going to try to illustrate them a little further. To do that permit me to use the analogy of an airplane and to recite a personal experience. In that we shall find a very apt illustration of all three of these great truths of Sant Mat.

A dead motor over mountain ranges
I used to do considerable flying. I had some airplanes of my own and gained a little skill in flying them. On one occasion, I was crossing the Siskiyou mountain range in northern California, sailing along at an altitude of almost two miles above

sea level. Those snow-covered summits and deep gorges, gigantic rocks and vast forests, all lay unrolling beneath me in a gorgeous panorama. Old Mount Shasta stood out to my left, and its twelve-thousand-foot peak I could almost have touched, if my arm had been a little longer. Here and there miles of billowy clouds crept lazily along the mountainsides, far below me, shining white in the morning sun. I was enjoying the flight with superb delight. I felt almost as if I were floating through the sunlit skies sustained by the everlasting arms. There was no thought of danger to myself. I was exultingly happy.

Then all of a sudden my motor went dead. No amount of coaxing could restore it to action. It was dead, hopelessly out. I looked around in every direction, but no place to land without a crash. Nothing as far as I could see—nothing but rocks and deep gorges and dense forests. Only one thing was now certain: beyond peradventure I must soon come down to earth. Even the minutes allotted to me were counted, and only my gliding angle was left—eleven times the distance I was above the ground—and then I must come down to earth, whether I was ready or not.

But how to make a satisfactory landing when there was no place to land? I continued to glide and look for an opening, or as the flyers say, an out. Miles went by under me, and all the while I was slowly but inevitably descending. The pull of gravity was as relentless as death itself and held its victim as surely within its grasp. Finally, far to the east, perhaps six miles, I saw a field and headed for it. Shortly reaching it, I circled the field twice to pick out the best approach, skimmed over the tops of some trees, side-slipped her down to break the too-rapid landing speed, and then set her down in that little field, none the worse for my dead motor.

Now, here is the point. The airplane is the human body.

The pilot sitting in it is the soul. The motor is the Master, and the gasoline from which all power is derived is the sound current. The mountain range, with its stony crag, its deep cuts, vast forests and low-rolling clouds, is this earth, the realm of matter. And my home, lying some 150 miles to the south, may represent our eternal home in Sach Khand.

Let us now make the application, so that by all means we do not fail to get the fundamental ideas fixed in our consciousness. Presumably I was headed for my home, but now having no power to rise, because wholly disconnected from the source of power and being utterly unable to continue the journey, I was slowly sinking toward the earth. This is an exact parallel to our situation spiritually. It pictures the situation of the whole world. Each one rises but for a moment above the horizon of life, spends that moment wasting the small store of energy he has acquired in former lives, and then slowly sinks to earth, to die and be reborn in an endless chain of cause and effect called karma.

But there is one avenue of escape, and only one. If he is fortunate enough to meet a real Master, he may find the way out. The Master, like the motor in the plane, is the connecting link between the source of power and the individual soul. The source of power is the sound current and it is in all men, like the gasoline in the tank of the plane; but it is latent. To us it is practically useless, because without the Master its power is not available. Just as the plane needs the motor to convert the latent power of the gasoline into dynamic energy, so the soul must have the Master to connect it with the sound current and make its power available. This the Master does when he gives the disciple initiation.

From that moment on, the divine energy is available, whereas before it was latent and useless to the individual. As the plane begins to rise the moment the power of the motor is applied, so the soul begins to rise the moment it is connected with the sound current by the Master. But the man without a Master is exactly like the airplane without a motor. The utmost that he can do is to glide, and that for only a limited time. Most of the human race are simply gliders, momentary gliders, drifters. Nothing more. They have no independent motive power by which to rise.

Now, the pilot in a motorless plane may have all the technical knowledge in the world. He may know how to build airplanes. He may be a master of all the sciences. Yet as he sits there in that motorless plane, all he can do is glide a little way. Precisely the situation in which all men without a Master find themselves, no matter how wise and learned they may be. Search the hearts of the wisest and best of men, and ask them if they have power to do as they please. They will tell you that they are helpless gliders, with power only to modify their gliding a little.

In like manner, a man may have all the book learning in the world. He may have all the sciences of the world at his command. He may be able to quote verbatim every line of the Vedas, the Shastras, the Koran and the Bible—all of the sacred hymns and bibles of the world. But that knowledge will never enable him to overcome the downward pull of earth's influences. Knowledge can save no one from *chaurasi da chakar*—the inevitable wheel of birth and death, called the wheel of eighty-four. Only dynamic power can do that, and dynamic power is not inherent in knowledge itself.

Also, the pilot may be a model of moral perfection. He may be the most rigid of purists, the most punctilious of all in observing every moral precept, and he may spend all his days in prayers; yet sitting there in that motorless plane, he is as helpless as the boldest scoundrel. So the man of moral perfection is likewise helpless when it comes to rising against the downward pull of earth's dominant forces which lead him ultimately to death and rebirth. Without the Master, he also is helpless.

Again, the pilot may have all of the training and skill of a Lindberg; he may be the most efficient and keenly intellectual pilot that ever sat in a plane; and yet without the power of the motor, he must come down to earth. The utmost that he can hope to do is to glide for a little season, and if he has favorable winds, he may stay up a little longer than the other fellow who has less favorable winds and less skill. But the winds of fortune blow not in the favor of all men.

In the same way, a man may have attained the very acme of human culture. He may be a marvel of erudition. He may be the very flower of earth's super-refinement. He may contain within himself the combined mastership of all the fine arts. He may speak every known language. In a word, he may have reached the summit of all possible human culture and achievement; and yet all of that will never lift him above the downward pull of those currents which are an integral part of this earth life. With all of his erudition and culture, the utmost that he can hope to do, like the pilot in the motorless plane, is to drift along a little above the dark streams of earth's more sordid conditions. With the favorable winds of good fortune, he may glide on for a time; and at last all that his culture can do for him is help him pick out a more favorable landing from which to begin his next venture.

But the landing he must take. He has no choice. He has no independent power to ascend the skies and go on to his real home. He must return to earth and begin his struggle all over again. The wheel of birth and death must roll on forever, and he must pass under it. He is hopelessly bound to these regions of mind and matter, of pain and struggle. But the soul who has the help of a Master, and he alone, has the power to rise and free himself, to shake off the dust of earth forever and mount to his eternal home.

From this illustration, it would appear that it does not lie in the power of any human being, high or low, ignorant or cultured, vile or saintly, to free himself from the bonds of earth and rise into the regions of light. And that is exactly what all of the saints teach. It is a fact of experience, not a theory, and it is fundamental in their system.

The final triumph

But suppose that while that airplane is gliding along over the mountains, slowly descending for the inevitable landing, suppose that the motor suddenly springs to life again. Once more the power is applied to the propeller, and the throb of life is again felt through every wire and rib, to the tips of her wings. We begin to rise. Oh, the glory of it! Only those who have had the experience may ever know what joy the pilot feels when he hears again the blessed hum of that motor and feels his ship begin to climb once more. The earth drops away beneath him and he triumphantly ascends the shining path of the skies. The old earth may now pull all she pleases, but there is a power within which is able to overcome the downward drag. So he climbs higher and higher, breathing the purer air of those upper regions, until at last he beholds his home on the distant horizon.

Just so is the joy of him who begins to hear the sweet sounds of the divine current within, when he feels a new power throbbing through every fiber of his being. He is now conscious of rising above all downward tendencies, thrilled with a sense of well-being which he never knew before. His real home, in the land of pure spirit, is even now on the horizon, and soon his feet will step upon its golden sands.

Addresses for Information and Books

INDIAN SUB-CONTINENT

INDIA
The Secretary
Radha Soami Satsang Beas
P.O. Dera Baba Jaimal Singh 143204
District Amritsar, Punjab

NEPAL
Mr. Dal Bahadur Shreshta
Radha Soami Satsang Beas
P. O. Box 1646, Gongabu, Dhapasi
Kathmandu

PAKISTAN
Mr. Dileep Kumar
18 B Lalazar, New Queens Road
Karachi, Sindh

SRI LANKA
Mr. Chandroo Mirpuri
39/3 Horton Palce
Colombo 7

SOUTHEAST ASIA

FOR FAR EAST
Mrs. Cami Moss
RSSB-HK
T.S.T., P.O. Box 90745
Kowloon, Hong Kong

MALAYSIA
Mr. Selvarajoo Pragasam
No. 15 Jalan SL 10/4
Bandar Sg. Long
43000 Kajang

THAILAND
Mr. Harmahinder Singh Sethi
58/32 Rachdapitsek Road, Soi 16
Thapra, Bangkok Yai 10600

INDONESIA
Mr. Ramesh Sadarangani
Jalan Pasir Putih IV/16, Block E 4
Ancol Timur, Jakarta Utara 14430

PHILIPPINES
Mr. Kay Sham
Science of the Soul Study Center
Don Jesus Boulevard
Alabang Hills, Cupang 1771
Muntinlupa City, Metro Manila

SINGAPORE
Mrs. Asha Melwani
Radha Soami Satsang Beas Singapore
19 Amber Road, Singapore 439868

ASIA PACIFIC

AUSTRALIA
Mr. Pradeep Raniga
P.O. Box 642
Balwyn North, Victoria 3104

NEW ZEALAND
Mr. Tony Waddicor
Science of the Soul Study Centre
P. O. Box 5331
Auckland

GUAM
Mrs. Hoori M. Sadhwani
115 Alupang Cove
241 Condo Lane, Tamuning 96911

HONG KONG
Mr. Manoj Sabnani
RSSB-HK, 3rd Floor, Eader Centre39-
41 Hankow Road,
Tsim Sha Tsui, Kowloon

JAPAN
Mr. Jani G. Mohinani
Radha Soami Satsang Beas
1-2-18 Nakajimadori
Aotani, Chuo-Ku
Kobe 651-0052

SOUTH KOREA,
TAIWAN, R.O.C.
Mr. Haresh Buxani
3rd floor, Eader Centre
39-41 Hankow Road
Tsim Sha Tsui
Kowloon, Hong Kong

NORTH AMERICA

CANADA
Mr. John Abel
#701-1012 Beach Avenue
Vancouver, B.C. V6E 1T7

Mrs. Meena Khanna
149 Elton Park Road
Oakville, Ontario L6J 4C2

MEXICO
Dr. Hector Esponda
RSSB-Mexico
Circuito Universidad 360
(In front of Vista Vallarta Golf Club)
Puerto Vallarta, Jalisco 48290

UNITED STATES
Mr. Hank Muller
1900 North Loop West, Suite 500
Houston, TX 77018

Dr. Vincent P. Savarese
2550 Pequeno Circle
Palm Springs, CA 92264

Science of the Soul Study Center
2415 East Washington Street
Petaluma, CA 94954

Dr. John Templer
114 Verdier Road
Beaufort, SC 29902-5440

Science of the Soul Study Center
4115 Gillespie Street
Fayetteville, NC 28306-9053

Dr. Frank E. Vogel
71 Old Farm Road
Concord, MA 01742

CARIBBEAN

FOR CARIBBEAN
Mr. Sean Finnigan
P. O. Box 2314
Port-au-Prince
Haiti, W. I.

BARBADOS
Mr. Deepak Nebhani
Radha Soami Satsang Beas
Lot No. 10, 5th Avenue
Belleville, St. Michael
Barbados, W. I.

CURACAO
Mr. Frank Claessen
La Quinta Villas 121
St. Catharina
Curacao, N. A.

GUYANA
Mrs. Rajni B. Manglani
A-80 Eping Avenue,
Bel Air Park,
Georgetown, Guyana

JAMAICA
Mrs. Shammi Khiani
P. O. Box 22
Montego Bay
Jamaica, W. I.

ST. MAARTEN
Mrs. Kanchan Mahbubani
R.S.S.B. Foundation
P. O. Box 978
Phillipsburg
St. Maarten, N. A.

SURINAME
Mr. Chandru Samtani
15 Venus Straat
Paramaribo
Suriname

TRINIDAD
Mr. Chandru Chatlani
20 Admiral Court
Westmoorings-by-Sea
Westmoorings
Trinidad, W. I.

CENTRAL AMERICA

BELIZE
Mrs. Chand Babani
5789 Goldson Avenue, Belize City

PANAMA
Mr. Deepak Dhanani
Altos Del Bosque
Residencial El Doral, Casa 195
Republica De Panama

SOUTH AMERICA

FOR SOUTH AMERICA
Mr. Hiro W. Balani
P.O. Box 486,
Malaga 29012, Spain

ARGENTINA
Mrs. Fabiana Shilton
Leiva 4363
Post Code 1427 Buenos Aires

BRAZIL
Mr. Willefort Leao
Rua Plinio Moscoso 1248
Edif. Sol de Verao, Apt. 201
40155-190, Salvador

CHILE
Mr. Vijay Harjani
Cosmos International S. A.
Manzana 5, Sitio 3
Iquique

COLOMBIA
Mrs. Emma Orozco
Calle 45, #99-25, Medellin

ECUADOR
Dr. Fernando Flores Villalva
Radha Soami Satsang Beas-Ecuador
Calle Marquez de Varela
Oe 3-68y Ave. America
P.O. Box 17-21-115, Quito

PERU
Mr. Carlos Fitts Villalva
P.O. Box 180658
Rinconada del Lago
1016-201 Lima

VENEZUELA
Mr. Jose Penaherrera
Calle "A", Residencias
Minarete, 9° Piso, Apto
91B, Urb.La Alameda,
Stafe, Caracas 1080

EUROPE

AUSTRIA
Mr. Hansjorg Hammerer
Sezenweingasse 10, Salzburg A-5020

BELGIUM
Mr. Piet J. E. Vosters
Driezenstraat 26
Turnhout 2300

BULGARIA
Mr. Emilio Saev
Foundation Radha Soami Satsang Beas
Bulgaria
P. O. Box 39, 8000 Bourgas

CYPRUS
Mr. Heraclis Achilleos
P. O. Box 29077, Nicosia 1035

CZECH REPUBLIC
Mr. Vladimir Skalsky
Maratkova 916,
420 00 Prague 411

DENMARK
Mr. Tony Sharma
Sven Dalsgaardsvej 33
DK-7430 Ikast

FINLAND
Ms. Anneli Wingfield
P. O. Box 1422
00101 Helsinki

FRANCE
Ct. Pierre de Proyart
7 Quai Voltaire,
Paris 75007

GERMANY
Mr. Rudolf Walberg
P. O. Box 1544
D-65800 Bad Soden / Taunus

GIBRALTAR
Mr. Sunder Mahtani
RSSB Charitable Trust Gibraltar
15 Rosia Road

GREECE
Mrs. Eleftheria Tsolaki
P.O. Box 35
Paleo Faliro 17503, Athens

ITALY
Mrs. Wilma Salvatori Torri
Via Bacchiglione 3, 00199 Rome

*THE NETHERLANDS
(HOLLAND)*
Radha Soami Satsang Beas - Nederland
Middenweg 145 E
1394 AH Nederhorst den Berg

NORWAY
Mr. Sohan Singh Mercy
St. Halvardsgt. 6
N-3015 Drammen

POLAND
Mr. Vinod Sharma
ul. 1go Sierpnia 36 B M-100
PL-02-134 Warszawa, Warsaw

PORTUGAL
Mrs. Sharda Lodhia
Rua Quinta Das Palmeiras, Lote 68
11° andar C, Oeiras 2780-145

ROMANIA
Mrs. Carmen Cismas
C.P. 6-12, Braila-810600

SLOVENIA
Mr. Marko Bedina
Brezje pri Trzicu 68, 4290 Trzic

SPAIN
Mr. J. W. Balani
Calle Panorama no. 15
Cerrado de Calderon
Malaga 29018

SWEDEN
Mr. Lennart Zachen
Norra Sonnarpsvägen 29
S-286 72 Asljunga

SWITZERLAND
Mr. Sebastian Zust-Bischof
Weissenrainstrasse 48
CH 8707 Uetikon am See (ZH)

UNITED KINGDOM
Mr. Narinder Singh Johal
Haynes Park Estate
Haynes, Bedford MK45 3BL

AFRICA

BENIN
Mr. Jaikumar T. Vaswani
01 Boite Postale 951,
Recette Principale, Cotonou

BOTSWANA
Dr. Krishan Lal Bhateja
P. O. Box 402539, Gaborone

GHANA
Mr. Murli Chatani
Radha Soami Satsang Beas
P. O. Box 3976, Accra

IVORY COAST
Mr. Konan N'Dri
08 Boite Postale 569
Abidjan 08

KENYA
Mr. Surinder Singh Ghir
P. O. Box 15134,
Langata 00509, Nairobi

LESOTHO
Mr. Sello Wilson Moseme
P. O. Box 750
Leribe 300

LIBYA (G.S.P.L.A.J.)
Mr. Roshan Lal
P.O. Box 38930, Bani Walid

MAURITIUS
Dr. I. Fagoonee
17 Manick Avenue
La Louise,
Quatre Bornes

NAMIBIA
Mrs. Jennifer Mary Carvill
P. O. Box 1258
Swakopmund 9000

NIGERIA
Mr. Nanik N. Balani
P.O. Box 5054, Lagos

RÉUNION
Ms. Marie-Lynn Marcel
5 Chemin 'Gonneau
Bernica, St Paul 97435

SIERRA LEONE
Mr. Kishore S. Mahboobani
82/88 Kissy Dock Yard,
P O Box 369, Freetown

SOUTH AFRICA
Mr. Gordon Clive Wilson
P. O. Box 47182, Greyville 4023

RSSB - SA
P.O. Box 5270
Cresta 2118

SWAZILAND
Mr. Peter Dunseith
P. O. Box 423, Mbabane

TANZANIA
Mr. D.N. Pandit
P.O. Box 1963
Dar-Es-Salaam

UGANDA
Mr. Sylvester Kakooza
Radha Soami Satsang Beas
P. O. Box 31381, Kampala

ZAMBIA
Mr. Chrispin Lwali
P.O. Box 12094
Chingola

ZIMBABWE
Mr. G.D. Wright
Pharmanova, P. O. Box 1726, Harare

MIDDLE EAST

BAHRAIN
Mr. Mangat Rai Rudra
Flat No. 12 Building No. 645
Road No. 2107
Manama 321

ISRAEL
Mr. Michael Yaniv
Moshav Sde Nitzan
D.N. Hanegev 85470

KUWAIT
Mr. Vijay Kumar
P. O. Box 1913, 13020 Safat

U.A.E.
Mr. Mohanlal Badlani
R.S.S.B. P.O. Box 37816,
Dubai

BOOKS ON THIS SCIENCE

SOAMI JI MAHARAJ
Sar Bachan Prose
Sar Bachan Poetry (Selections)

BABA JAIMAL SINGH
Spiritual Letters (to Hazur Maharaj Sawan Singh: 1896-1903)

MAHARAJ SAWAN SINGH
The Dawn of Light (letters to Western disciples: 1911-1934)
Discourses on Sant Mat
My Submission (introduction to *Philosophy of the Masters*)
Philosophy of the Masters (*Gurmat Sidhant*), in 5 volumes
    (an encyclopedia on the teachings of the Saints)
Spiritual Gems (letters to Western disciples: 1919-1948)
Tales of the Mystic East (as narrated in satsangs)

MAHARAJ JAGAT SINGH
The Science of the Soul (discourses and letters: 1948-1951)

MAHARAJ CHARAN SINGH
Die to Live (answers to questions on meditation)
Divine Light (discourses and letters: 1959-1964)
Light on Saint John
Light on Saint Matthew
Light on Sant Mat (discourses and letters: 1952-1958)
The Master Answers (to audiences in America: 1964)
The Path (first part of *Divine Light*)
Quest for Light (letters: 1965-1971)
Spiritual Discourses, in 2 volumes
Spiritual Heritage (from tape-recorded talks)
Thus Saith the Master (to audiences in America: 1970)

BOOKS ABOUT THE MASTERS
Call of the Great Master—Diwan Daryai Lal Kapur
Heaven on Earth—Diwan Daryai Lal Kapur
Treasure Beyond Measure—Shanti Sethi
With a Great Master in India—Julian P. Johnson
With the Three Masters, in 3 volumes—from the diary of
    Rai Sahib Munshi Ram

INTRODUCTION TO SPIRITUALITY

A Spiritual Primer—Hector Esponda Dubin
Honest Living: A Means to an End—M. F. Singh
The Inner Voice—Colonel C. W. Sanders
Liberation of the Soul—J. Stanley White
Life is Fair: The Law of Cause and Effect—Brian Hines

BOOKS ON MYSTICISM

A Treasury of Mystic Terms, Part I: The Principles of Mysticism
    (6 volumes)—John Davidson
The Holy Name: Mysticism in Judaism—Miriam Caravella
Yoga and the Bible—Joseph Leeming

BOOKS ON SANT MAT IN GENERAL

In Search of the Way—Flora E. Wood
Living Meditation: A Journey beyond Body and Mind
    —Hector Esponda Dubin
Message Divine—Shanti Sethi
The Mystic Philosophy of Sant Mat—Peter Fripp
Mysticism, The Spiritual Path, in 2 volumes—Lekh Raj Puri
The Path of the Masters—Julian P. Johnson
Radha Soami Teachings—Lekh Raj Puri
A Soul's Safari—Netta Pfeifer

MYSTICS OF THE EAST SERIES

Bulleh Shah—J. R. Puri and T. R. Shangari
Dadu, The Compassionate Mystic—K. N. Upadhyaya
Dariya Sahib, Saint of Bihar—K. N. Upadhyaya
Guru Nanak, His Mystic Teachings—J. R. Puri
Guru Ravidas, The Philosopher's Stone—K. N. Upadhyaya
Kabir, The Great Mystic—Isaac A. Ezekiel
Kabir, The Weaver of God's Name—V. K. Sethi
Mira, The Divine Lover—V. K. Sethi
Saint Namdev—J. R. Puri and V. K. Sethi
Saint Paltu—Isaac A. Ezekiel
Sarmad, Martyr to Love Divine—Isaac A. Ezekiel
Sultan Bahu—J. R. Puri and K. S. Khak
Tukaram, The Ceaseless Song of Devotion—C. Rajwade
Tulsi Sahib, Saint of Hathras—J. R. Puri and V. K. Sethi